READY-TO-USE

Fundamental Motor Skills & Movement Activities

for

Young Children

Teaching, Assessment & Remediation

Joanne M. Landy
& Keith R. Burridge

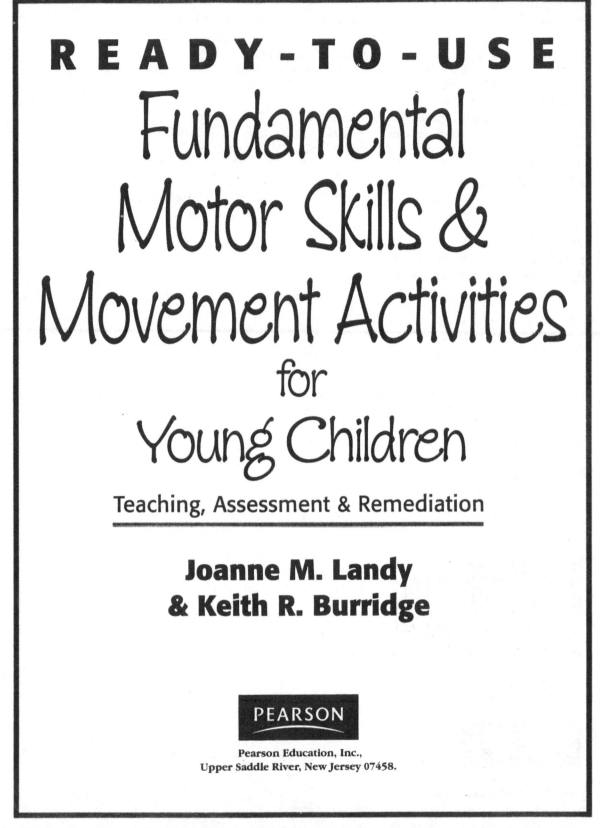

PEARSON

Pearson Education, Inc.,
Upper Saddle River, New Jersey 07458.

COMPLETE MOTOR SKILLS ACTIVITIES PROGRAM

Library of Congress Cataloging-in-Publication Data

Landy, Joanne M.
   Ready-to-use fundamental motor skills & movement activities for
young children: Teaching, assessment & remediation / Joanne M. Landy,
Keith R. Burridge ; illustrations by Joanne M. Landy.
     p.   cm. — (Complete Motor Skills Activities Program)
   Includes bibliographical references (p.).
   ISBN 0-13-013941-6
    1. Movement education.   2. Motor learning.   3. Education,
Elementary—Activity programs.   I. Burridge, Keith R.   II. Title.
III. Series: Landy, Joanne M. Complete Motor Skills Activities
Program.
GV452.L355   1999
372.86—dc21   99–22410
                                                  CIP

Acquisitions Editor: *Susan Kolwicz*
Production Editor: *Mariann Hutlak*
Interior Design/Formatter: *Dee Coroneos*

© 1999 *by* Joanne M. Landy and Keith R. Burridge

Printed in the United States of America

15, 14, 13, 12

ISBN 0-13-013941-6

ISBN-13: 978-0-13-013941-2
ISBN-10:   0-13-013941-6

9 780130 139412

90000

FAMILY EDUCATION
NETWORK

PEARSON

www.pearsonhighered.com

DEDICATION

To our children,
Max, Jr. and Nikki (Joanne's)
&
Adam and Dane (Keith's),
who have all suffered the loss of a parent.
Thank you for your love and support.

ABOUT THE AUTHORS

Joanne M. Landy earned a B.Ed. degree, graduating with Great Distinction from the University of Regina, Saskatchewan, Canada in 1974. She also completed a post graduate international P.E. study course through Concordia University in Montreal, Quebec, and a Personal Trainer course through Renouf Fitness Academy in Perth.

Joanne's professional background includes 10 years of secondary teaching in physical education/health and mathematics; 10 years of specialist teaching in primary physical education, as well as several years of University demonstration teaching in P.E. methodology and pedagogy programs, in the Canadian school system. In 1988 Joanne and her late husband, Professor Maxwell Landy, were part of the leadership team at the National Youth Foundation Fitness Camp in Los Angeles. She is also co-author with Maxwell of the four-book series *Complete Physical Education Activities Program* (Parker Publishing, 1993).

Joanne now resides with her children in Perth and operates a Lifestyle Education consulting business which provides in–depth workshops and inservicing in physical education at all levels, including University P.E. teacher training programs. She is also a member of the Board of Consultants for Sportsmart/Sportime Australia (Melbourne-based), which markets a wide range of innovative and educational manipulative equipment in physical education. In the recreational areas, Joanne has been instrumental in developing and coordinating youth activity-based programs which include a Junior Basketball Skills Development Program, a "Tune-Up-Kids" program for young children from 5–12 years of age which focuses on development of fundamental movement skills, and a personal development program for teenage girls (13–18 years of age) called "On the Move." She has also set up "Tune Up" programs for adults and runs team-building and motivational sessions for school staffs, corporate business groups, and other community groups.

Joanne has presented at major HPERD (Health, Physical Education, Recreation and Dance) conferences in North America, Australia, and New Zealand. She also has facilitated many workshops in primary/secondary P.E. teaching at the University of Western Australia, Notre Dame College of Education, Western Washington University, Washington State, University of Regina, Saskatchewan, and major university centers throughout New Zealand. This year, Joanne lectured at Murdoch University, Education Faculty, in the Primary Physical Education teacher training program. She maintains an active lifestyle and is still involved in many sports on a regular basis.

Keith R. Burridge earned a Dip. Ed. from Nedlands Secondary Teachers College, followed by a B.P.E. degree (1978) and M.Ed. from the University of Western Australia, Perth. Keith's professional background includes 15 years as a secondary physical education and science teacher, 5 years as a primary physical education specialist, and 4 years of special education working with children with movement difficulties. From

1995–97 he was employed by the Department of Education of Western Australia (Perth) as a school Development Officer in Physical Education and was responsible for professional development in P.E. for over 80 schools. He has represented Australia at the elite level in canoeing.

Keith was one of the key writers for the Western Australia Department of Education's 1998 Fundamental Movement Skills Package. He has lectured at Notre Dame College of Education and Murdoch University, and facilitated programs for early childhood education. Keith has presented F.M.S. and best practices in teaching workshops throughout Western Australia. He is the co-author with Joanne Landy of the newly released book *50 Simple Things You Can Do to Raise a Child Who is Physically Fit* (Macmillan, 1997). As a F.M.S. specialist, Keigh has contributed in the writing of a book called *Why Bright Children Fail* (Hammond, 1996). He is also the designer for a K-3 computer assessment package for identifying children at an early age who have coordination problems. This program is in operation in over 400 schools in Western Australia.

Presently, Keith is teaching at Willeton Senior High School in Perth and piloting a special program to work with children at educational risk.

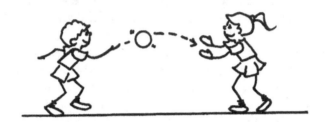

ACKNOWLEDGMENT

The authors would like to acknowledge the assistance of Dr. Dawne Larkin and Beth Hands for allowing adaptation of their fundamental movement skill checklists.

Thanks also to Beth Hands for her valuable contribution to aspects of the book.

INTRODUCTION TO COMPLETE MOTOR SKILLS ACTIVITIES PROGRAM

The *Complete Motor Skills Activities Program* consists of three books:

➤ Ready-to-Use Fundamental Motor Skills & Movement Activities
  for Young Children

➤ Ready-to-Use Fine Motor Skills & Handwriting Activities for Young Children

➤ Ready-to-Use Motor Skills & Movement Station Lesson Plans for Young Children

This program has been designed as a motor skills program for teachers, professionals, and parents in related fields (remedial, rehabilitation, and medical areas), working in the school environment, the home environment, or the community environment to assist children who have coordination difficulties in the performance and mastering of fundamental movement skills.

The focus of this program is to provide enjoyable developmentally-appropriate movement experiences in the teaching of these fundamental movement skills so that the children gain both competence and confidence in successfully performing these skills.

We emphasize that if the strategies are to be successful, teachers and parents need to be aware that although children may be able to perform the tasks adequately in terms of task completion, focus must be directed to *how* the task is completed; that is, focus must be directed toward quality of the movement—not just the outcome of the movement.

FUNDAMENTAL MOVEMENT SKILLS

Fundamental Movement Skills (FMS) are gross motor movements that involve different body parts such as feet, legs, trunk, head, arms, and hands. FMS are the foundation movements for more complex and specialized skills required to play low-organized games, sports, gymnastics, dance, and recreational activities. These skills can be categorized into three main skill areas:

1. *Body management skills* involve controlling body balance whether on the move (dynamic balance) such as rolling, stopping, landing, turning, twisting, bending, swinging, stretching, and dodging; or being stationary (static balance)

such as balancing on one foot. Body management skills also include awareness of body parts, and how the body moves in personal and general space.

2. *Locomotion skills* are movements that take the body in any direction, from one point to another. Locomotion skills should be learned from an early age onwards, and include walking, running, dodging, jumping and landing, hopping, leaping, skipping, and sliding.

3. *Object-control skills* involve hand-eye or foot-eye coordination in manipulation of such objects as balls, hoops, jump ropes, racquets, bats, and hockey sticks. They involve underhand throwing, overhand throwing, catching, bouncing, dribbling, rolling, striking skills with one or both hands, and kicking and trapping skills.

Motor memory is also an important component to this learning process and relates to the child's ability to visually and auditorially copy single movements, movement patterns, and rhythm patterns.

Current research suggests that if children do not reach a degree of competence and confidence in fundamental movement skills by the sixth grade, they will not engage in regular physical activity or sports for the rest of their lives.

SEVEN ESSENTIAL KEYS

Successful skills teaching in fundamental movement skills can result if you incorporate the following seven essential keys:

1. *Show enthusiasm, care, and interest.* These are qualities that cannot be written into any program. They come from *you,* and without them the program is not going to be so effective as it could be.

2. *Use visual demonstration with instruction* whenever possible. You may even need to physically move the child through some of the actions.

3. *Give praise, encouragement, and feedback.* These are an essential part of the learning process. Simply to say "do your best" does not bring about a constructive change. What is needed is good information about techniques and feedback (information about what the child has done). For example, "I watched the way you held the ball correctly in your fingers" or "That was a great effort; this time let's put your other foot forward."

4. *Create a positive, fun learning environment.* Sometimes we get preoccupied with telling the child what he or she is doing wrong or what he or she has not done instead of focusing on what he or she should be doing. A positive comment indicates to a child approval; the child can then develop trust and a willingness to keep trying.

5. *Keep the information simple and easy to follow.* Teaching by small-step progression is ideal. Progress may be a lot slower than you think and so patience definitely becomes a virtue.

6. ***Keep the home play sessions shorter, more frequent, yet allowing for ample practice.*** Some parents may be too enthusiastic and make the session simply too long. By keeping the sessions shorter, you can ensure that physical and mental fatigue do not become a factor and that the child's interest level is sustained.

7. ***Avoid showing frustration; be patient.*** If *you* feel frustrated, imagine how the child must feel. Frustration on your part is easily picked up by the child and compounds difficulties. Try saying "I think this is a good place to stop for today. Let's continue tomorrow."

ABOUT THIS BOOK

Each section is comprised of four areas: Teaching Points, Skill Activity Progressions, Related Games or Challenges, and Common Faults. The Contents gives the approximate age level for teaching these skills. Children may display difficulties with selected skills or may have difficulties in many areas of movement. In either case, this book will assist each child to improve his or her coordination skills. If the child experiences no movement difficulties, this book is still a valuable resource to promote correct skills and provide valuable play and learning time with other children.

➤ *Teaching Points:* These consist of "Preparing to Move" points; "Moving" points; and "Teachable Points" and Common Faults. The teachable points and common faults are also presented in Section 5 in a form where they can be cut and pasted onto cardboard to become pointer cards. Place teachable points on one side of the card and common faults on the other side. It is strongly recommended that teachers as well as parents do this to assist in their teaching.

➤ *Skill Activity Progressions:* The activities have been arranged in a suggested teaching order. You will need to find at what activity stage the child is by going through each stage. Remember, we are concerned with the *quality* of the movement. Do not try to move to the next activity until the previous one is mastered.

➤ *Related Games and Challenges:* Following the activity progressions are suggestions for games or extensions of the progressions in the form of challenges that further reinforce the skill(s) being learned. This is the fun aspect of learning the skill, and should always be included in sessions with the child.

➤ *Common Faults:* Listed here are some "commonalities" of incorrect movement for you to be aware of as you observe the child's performance. However, we emphasize that you focus on and provide feedback that is positive, rather than dwelling on everything that is "wrong." A unique feature of this book is that each common fault is specifically addressed by providing several activities that the child can practice and master through small-step progression.

➤ *Skill Pointer Cards:* These consist of key teaching points for each movement area and the common faults for that skill, and are placed in Section 5 to become a hands-on reference.

Knowing that children need to be given the best possible start to life and learning, we recommend this book as a valuable resource to achieve this goal. Children move to learn, but first of all, they must learn to move!

Joanne M. Landy & Keith R. Burridge

CONTENTS

SECTION 1
FITNESS AWARENESS

SECTION 2
BODY CONTROL SKILLS

SECTION 3
LOCOMOTION SKILLS

SECTION 4
OBJECT-CONTROL SKILLS

SECTION 5
POINTER NOTES AND POINTER CUE CARDS FOR TEACHABLE POINTS AND COMMON FAULTS

USING THIS BOOK

Before taking the child through each of the skill activities and games, read the following section carefully. The suggestions will assist you in your teaching strategies.

We suggest that you follow a format called "START":

S: Start with the first activity and progress through each one.

T: Teach the necessary points relevant to each activity.

A: Assess whether the child can complete the requirements of the activity (both successful technique as well as outcome). This can take as little as a few minutes for each activity.

R: Reteach any previously taught techniques that are not being successfully performed. Assess again and, if the activity is being performed correctly, move onto the next activity.

T: Try to vary the sessions by mixing the activities with the games suggested and add your own games, if possible.

We strongly recommend that you *first* teach non-moving parts of a skill and *then* the moving parts.

During the practicing of the activity you need to observe two things:

1. Is the outcome successful, or what level of success is achieved?

2. Is the action being completed correctly.?

It is important that you look at how the movement is being done. For example, a young child may throw a ball accurately to you with the incorrect foot forward and holding the ball in the palm of his or her hand. ***Why worry if a successful outcome is the result?*** In the case of the throw, as the demands for distance and accuracy increase and the pressures of a game are involved, poor technique will begin to limit success. **So, it's not just "do it," but let's "do it right!"**

GUIDELINES FOR TEACHING ACTIVITIES

"Activities" are of two types:

➤ Those that have an outcome as the goal.

➤ Those that have a teachable point as the goal.

GOAL: OUTCOME

Have the child complete the activity after you have visually (if possible) and verbally explained the activity. For example, let's take a hopping activity in which the child is required to jump from two feet and land and balance on one foot. **The goal is to land balanced on one foot.**

1. Have the child complete the activity.

2. Look at the outcome. (Did the child land on one foot and did he or she balance?)

3. *Answer "yes."* Check with your pointer card for the points dealing with the goal of the task. Did the child land on his or her forefoot? Was the head up and eyes focused forward? Did the child bend his or her knee on landing?

4. *Answer "yes."* Move on to the next activity.

5. If the outcome is successful but one or more of the movements are incorrect, then this becomes a *teachable moment and you explain and/or demonstrate what is required and have child practice that movement using the same activity.*

6. *Answer "no."* If the outcome is not successful, you will follow exactly the same format as explained in steps 3 and 5. Remember, correct one movement at a time.

7. If you cannot see what the child is doing incorrectly, look at the pointers on common faults to assist you.

Do not become frustrated if you cannot work out what the child is doing wrong. It is just as effective to go back and take the child through what he or she should be doing correctly!

GOAL: TEACHABLE POINT

Use an overarm throwing activity as an example, with the goal being to get the child to take a large backswing with his or her arm. Have the child take the ball with a correct grip and stand side-on to the target. Demonstrate the action first and then, without your assistance, call **"Down as far as you can and back as far as you can."**

1. Have child complete the activity.

2. Did child do it correctly? (Did the child's arm extend down and back enough? Did his or her head stay still and eyes remain focused on the target?)

3. *Answer "yes."* Move on to the next activity.

4. *Answer "no."* You will probably need to demonstrate again and emphasize the points. You may need to physically take the child through the activity again.

The key to teaching the child is to take it slowly and do not try to teach too much at once.

GUIDELINES FOR TEACHING RELATED GAMES

Use a related game at the end of an activity session or in place of activity sessions. The game can provide an enjoyable and social experience for the child. You can still give "tips" on technique but only as passing remarks as the emphasis is on enjoyment, not teaching. Observe the child at play. The mistakes that are made by the child and are obvious can be dealt with in an activity session.

We emphasize one more point. Do not be restricted by the activities and games in this program. If you can think of additional activities or games, then use them. However, bear in mind that the teachable points should still form the foundation of your instruction.

CHILDREN WILL DEVELOP SKILLS IF YOU ENSURE THEY ARE GIVEN:

- ☞ Good technique provided by teachable points.
- ☞ Sufficient time to practice.
- ☞ Enjoyable and positive experiences/motivation.

We recommend that if the child is experiencing movement difficulties, commence with motor memory, body image, and spatial awareness activities first. When the child displays competence and confidence in these areas, move on to the other movement sections.

GENERAL ASSESSMENT INFORMATION

Assessment is an important part of any teaching program as it gives an insight into the strengths and weaknesses of a child's movement skills and, therefore, provides a starting point for instruction. Logically, when providing an enrichment program for a child, the criteria that are not yet developed *and* have the greatest impact on the skill outcome should be taught or corrected first.

For classroom teachers, it is useful to obtain a class profile that will indicate if there are common problems that need to be taught or corrected. Fortunately, there are now computer programs that produce recorded and graphical information of class and individual profiles as well as generate individual reports, class records, and activities for individual criteria that have yet to be achieved or developed.

The assessment technique suggested in this book is qualitative and is intended to provide a guideline to how movement skills may be assessed. Each section contains information on assessment.

Practice in movement observation is essential and it may take time to develop confidence and competence. Persevere and be patient as you will find that observational skills are not only essential for assessment, but also for successful teaching.

Note: These are only guidelines, you may wish to develop your own method of observation and recording.

EXPLANATION OF ASSESSMENT SCORING METHOD

Outcome/Appearance

Look at the child performing the skill and try to visualize if the movement looks correct. This will be partly determined by experience, but you will be amazed how quickly your observational skills will improve over a short time.

The overall description is based on a combination of four factors:

1. The success of the outcome—has the child caught the ball? Remained balanced?

2. The consistency of the performance

3. The rhythm of the action, so important for successful movement

4. Coordination—do the parts work together as a whole in the correct sequence?

For the **Outcome/Appearance** it is suggested that a **3-point** scale be used. This is only a recommendation and individual preferences are acceptable. The scoring system is as follows:

Score 3 **If achieved.** (The movement is performed competently.)

Score 2 **If almost achieved.** (The movement is not refined, but is present.)

Score 1 **If not yet achieved/developed.** (The movement has not developed adequately.)

On each of the assessment sheets there are examples of skill interpretation that should improve understanding of this suggested assessment method. Here is an example of Outcome/Appearance from:

KICKING FOR ACCURACY

Outcome/Appearance

Score 3 If kick is relatively well struck, looks rhythmical, and goes through the markers. **(Achieved)**

Score 2 If kick is relatively well struck but does not have consistency in accuracy. **(Almost achieved)**

Score 1 If kicking action lacks rhythm and the result is poorly struck and consistently inaccurate. **(Not yet achieved/developed)**

The assessment of individual criteria is based on exactly the same 3-point scale as that used for **Outcome/Appearance.** Here is an example of **Individual Criteria** assessment from:

KICKING FOR ACCURACY

Assessment of Individual Criteria

Outcome/ Appearance • Success • Consistency • Rhythm • Coordination	1. Eyes focused on ball source.	2. Step forward with non-kicking foot.	3. Adequate backswing of kicking leg.	4. Ball contacted inside of kicking foot.	5. Balance maintained throughout kicking action.	6. Good extension in follow-through in direction of target.

2. Step forward with non-kicking foot.

Score 3 On this movement if the non-kicking foot achieves this move the majority of the time. **(Achieved)**

Score 2 On this movement if the non-kicking foot achieves this move, but it is inconsistent. **(Almost achieved)**

Score 1 On this movement if the non-kicking foot fails to achieve this move, that is, the incorrect foot or no movement occurs. **(Not yet achieved/developed)**

IMPORTANT FACTS FOR PARENTS TO KNOW

➤ Have reasonable expectations for your child's abilities and for potential skill changes.

➤ Children with movement difficulties often do not learn so well or so quickly using conventional methods of instruction as do coordinated children.

➤ Be aware that children experiencing movement difficulties require longer to learn a skill. They need constant feedback and quite often require kinesthetic assistance; that is, they must be physically taken through movements.

➤ Be aware that some difficulties will disappear with maturity; others will not. The longer we leave physical problems, the harder they are to correct because the children practice poor movements that become habits and then these have to be undone. Also if these difficulties are left too long, some children begin to display avoidance behavior.

➤ Because the identification of physical problems can be achieved early, the prognosis for improvement is favorable, but requires consistent, cooperative, and effective intervention by parents, schools and coaches.

➤ Make your child as independent as possible. To do this, you must resist the temptation to complete tasks for your son or daughter, including such daily requirements as tying shoelaces, cutting food, and dressing. Be there to assist your child to complete these tasks, but promote independence.

➤ If your child does have a specific weakness in one or two areas, try to spend three 15-minute sessions per week focusing on these areas of weakness in addition to the normal home play. (This is only a recommended time allocation. You have to fit in sessions to suit your individual situation.)

➤ It is very important to promote the strengths of the children as well as assisting with their difficulties. This can be achieved by choosing some of the activities that you know your child is good at. For example, your child may have difficulties with catching but be great at kicking, so do some kicking sessions or include kicking in a remediation session.

Be patient because it does take longer for children to learn skills than we think. Praise your child's efforts, as we all need encouragement. Try to be consistent in following this program.

ANALYZING MOVEMENT

In analyzing movement we need to realize and identify the common characteristics of these movements. Once these common elements are understood, the task of analysis becomes much easier. In fact, if you cannot recognize correct and incorrect movement, then it becomes difficult to *teach* movement. *(We suggest that you use the pointer cards whenever teaching.)*

When analyzing and teaching movement, start with the non-moving components and then progress to the moving components. The non-moving parts of a movement (the "set-up" or "ready position") set the stage for a successful movement performance.

The sequence for observing movement is:

➤ Position of the feet

➤ Legs and knees

➤ Hips

➤ Trunk

➤ Head

➤ Arms and hands

COMMON CHARACTERISTICS OF MOVEMENT

BALANCE

Balance is a component of movement that is essential for all movements. It is the foundation from which other movements are built. Without balance, many of the other components mentioned below cannot occur successfully because the body is no longer in the correct position to impart force and accuracy to the movement. Narrow stance and excessive head and body movements are common causes of poor balance.

HEAD STILL/STABLE

Like balance, this is an essential basic to successful movement. The head should provide the fulcrum from which other body parts move around. Once the head moves excessively, object focus, body positioning and balance are affected.

BODY ALIGNMENT

Fundamental movements—especially locomotor activities and target activities such as golf—require that the body is aligned to the target or the object that is being controlled moves in a straight line. Therefore, it is apparent that for maximum force, efficiency and accuracy, the body and its parts move in good alignment.

KNEES FLEXED

Having the knees slightly flexed increases balance, aids in maintaining body height, has a positive influence on weight and force transference in striking activities, promotes agility, and assists in cushioning movements such as landings. If the body height needs to be changed, it is usually achieved by flexing and extending the knees.

BODY HEIGHT CONSISTENCY

In many fundamental movements there is a requirement that the body posture remains relatively consistent. Excessive bending or straightening of the body affects balance and the body's spatial relationship to other objects. Usually the posture required in the non-moving position (or "ready" position) should be maintained throughout the movement. If body height needs to change, it is usually done so at the knees.

TRANSFERENCE OF WEIGHT AND FORCE

This is fundamental for gaining maximum efficiency and force in a movement. The correct sequence for weight transference in throwing and striking activities is onto the back foot in the backswing, and forward onto the front foot on the forward swing. Quite often transference occurs naturally as a consequence of correct movement sequences of the body parts. This concept is particularly important in locomotor, throwing, and striking activities.

EYES FOCUSED

Whether balancing, manipulating objects, or performing locomotor skills, to have the eyes focused on a target in a throwing activity or on a stationary fixed point while balancing remains key for successful performance.

EXTENSION AND FOLLOW-THROUGH

All throwing and striking activities require that the body parts extend to maximize the force applied to an object or, as in the case of jumping, to the ground. Extension achieved at the completion of a throw, kick, or strike is called follow-through and should be initially in the direction of the target. In the case of many throwing and striking activities, the follow-through continues around the body.

RHYTHM AND TIMING

Rhythm is the consequence of well-sequenced movements. Poor rhythm, along with an unsuccessful outcome, is the easiest way to detect that the skill has not been mastered and other movement components need to be monitored.

SUCCESSFUL OUTCOME

Quality of movement usually provides a successful outcome. However, a successful outcome for young children does not necessarily mean that the movement techniques are correct. Young children who are large or strong for their age can have successful outcomes in activities that measure time or distance, but achieve this with poor technique. We need to be aware of this fact. A successful outcome in movement that requires accuracy may be a more pertinent guide to correct technique.

Note: Strength, fitness, and flexibility are important physical attributes that, like coordination, contribute to success in physical activities. The child needs to be proficient in these areas; if a notable weakness is apparent, attention to improving these abilities is necessary.

Section 1

FITNESS AWARENESS

FITNESS AWARENESS

We cannot emphasize enough the importance of instilling in children at an early age the competence and confidence in movement that will enhance overall coordination, enjoyment of activity, and self-esteem. But equally as important is to focus on developing the child's overall fitness—including aerobic capacity, flexibility, strength, agility, alertness, and reaction—which is an important part of overall coordination!

Children who lack general overall coordination will not develop good fitness. These children do not have appropriate movement skills. For example, a child who cannot run properly, who keeps falling over or running into things and getting hurt, will be significantly hindered in his or her aerobic development.

A prerequisite to any fitness or activity program is that the child feels comfortable with moving. A child who does not like to be active, who finds movement difficult, will have a tendency to become overweight and lethargic, and have poor aerobic endurance and coordination problems.

Section 1 is devoted to providing "fit" guidelines and activities for the young child with movement difficulties. If children are exposed at an early age to quality, purposeful, interesting, and enjoyable exercises on a regular basis, then they should develop positive attitudes towards being active and pursuing an active lifestyle for the rest of their lives, and have the desire for regular activity as an adult. A regular dose of "fun exercise-type" activities will also affect a child's health, growth, motor skill development, and personal and social development. However, the activities must be appropriate to the age capabilities and developmental stages of the child.

"FIT" GUIDELINES

➤ *Observe the child at play.* Take a "mental snapshot"—is the child active? Energetic? Enthusiastic? Receptive? Responding positively to challenges? Showing enjoyment? Interacting with you and with others?

➤ *Make fitness fun!* Children are not mini-adults! They simply obtain their fitness by doing activities that they enjoy. Imposing "training" on them will only create an uphill battle of resistance.

➤ *Children do activity intermittently.* Remember that they tire easily, but recover quickly.

➤ *Play is the fundamental "key"* to life and contributes to the overall development of the child. Through "playful" experiences children can explore, create, express, discover, interact, and learn about the environment around them and about themselves. Play is about "promoting lifestyle activity for youth." Play is for adults participating in the lives of children!

➤ From an early age, *educate children about what it means to be "FIT":*

"F"—how often should we do activity? (*frequency*)

"I"—how much effort should be put into it? (*intensity*)

"T"—how long should we do the activity? (*time*)

"T"—what types of activity can we do? (*type*)

➤ *Moderate activity is valued and beneficial.* Active children become active adults. Any activity is better than no activity. Experts recommend that primary school-aged children accumulate at least 30–60 minutes of age- and developmentally-appropriate physical activity *daily!* Encourage more than 30–60 minutes; discourage extended periods of inactivity for children. Exposure to a variety of interesting, enjoyable, and beneficial activity at the developmentally-appropriate age level is highly recommended!

TWENTY EXERCISE RECOMMENDATIONS

1. Establish boundaries and mark them clearly for each activity session. Use such markers as witch's hats, domes, or throwing rings.

2. Establish a set of *signals* for starting, stopping, and movement. These signals will enhance children's listening skills, alertness and reaction, and spatial awareness. Practice these until the children can respond immediately.

3. Give instructions clearly and concisely. Demonstrate whenever possible.

4. Warm up gently and rhythmically, using as many of the major muscle groups as possible in the main activity. Begin in a slow, controlled manner, gradually increasing intensity.

5. Keep the warm-up simple. Use easy, "catchy" names that children will remember.

6. Identify the activities with names that children can easily remember and associate the movement with the name; for example, "Dead Bug"—children quickly and carefully drop to the floor on their backsides with limbs waving in the air.

7. Include specific stretching and movements that are used in the activities to follow.

8. Avoid tag-type games in the early part of the warm-up.

9. Modify and adapt according to age level, space available, and weather conditions.

10. Use music with a moderate, steady beat to enhance the enjoyment and rhythm of the movements.

11. Stretching activities can occur during the warm-up and then in the cool-down, but stretching activities should be performed while the muscles are still warm.

12. Cooling down is necessary to help the body return to its normal resting state and should be part of the overall fitness package. The activity is continued, but at a lower intensity.

13. Quiet, gentle background music could be used to help the children "unwind" and relax. Have each child concentrate on his or her breathing.

14. Be aware of children's growth and development. Movement is needed for the development of bones and muscles; therefore, it is important that children experience developmentally-appropriate activities for their age group.

15. Be a positive role model by being enthusiastic and joining in whenever and wherever possible. Children learn by example. Encourage, praise, and provide constructive feedback; don't push or be overbearing.

16. Provide a variety of activities. Make the activity fun, challenging, interesting, and motivating. Vary the intensity so that children do not become fatigued.

17. Be aware of exercise "do's" and "don'ts." Never stretch "cold" muscles. Avoid ballistic movements when stretching. Avoid exercises that hyperextend any joint areas. Children should be encouraged to use their own body weight to develop strength. (See page 17 for a description of the more common stretches that are no longer recognized as suitable for children, why they should be excluded, and alternative suggestions.)

18. See fitness as the BIG picture. That is, physical fitness is only one integral part of the total health and well-being package that also includes good nutrition, mental health (thinking), emotional health (attitude), quality sleep, relaxation, and "play" time. The key is to achieve a "balance" of all these health-related components!

19. Establish exercise/activity as a "habit." That is, establish an activity routine schedule, but within this schedule be flexible and realistic as you may not have the time or opportunity to do activity with the child at the same time each day.

20. Develop in the child a "knowing attitude"; that is, get the child used to being active, used to doing exercises, and in the know of *why* exercise is so good for you!

STRATEGIES TO ENCOURAGE THE RELUCTANT CHILD

➤ Try to discern *why* a child is reluctant to be active: Is she or he overweight? Is she or he insecure? Does the child have a low self-esteem? A fear of failure? Does the child feel unsafe? Does not want to get physically or emotionally hurt? Does the child have poor coordination?

➤ Create a safe, fun positive learning environment free of any physical threat, ridicule, bullying, put-downs.

➤ Provide immediate feedback, given out at the "time of doing." Use words of praise and encouragement that are meaningful: "You ran all the way without stopping—that's terrific!"

➤ Don't be overprotective. Establish consistency and firmness.

➤ Try to create situations that guarantee success within a short period of time.

➤ Keep within the limits of the child's abilities. Don't force the child to do the activity; instead, encourage the child to be responsible for her or his own activity involvement.

➤ From time to time, offer some kind of incentive or reward. The instant reward is praise and encouragement. Set a goal that is followed up by a reward: "If you can try to run for two minutes non-stop, then you can have free play with your favorite piece of equipment at the end!"

➤ Provide a variety of activity experiences that will sustain children's interest.

➤ Have the children create activities that the whole class can then do together. Include a description and even a drawing with the "title" of the activity.

➤ Don't confuse a child's *needs* with the child's *wants*. Young children do not have the knowledge or experience to know what is good for them. We need to impose our knowledge of the importance of exercise on the child and the benefits of regular play activity.

WARMING-UP ACTIVITIES

WARMING-UP SIGNALS

The following signals provide ways of effectively mobilizing children, and developing their listening skills and spatial awareness. Identify the boundaries of the play area that children will move around in. Use a minimum of 6–8 cone markers or witch's hats spaced evenly apart around the area. Establish the following signals that children can quickly learn and respond to. Single-out good listeners and praise them!

1. *Homes!* Find a home space in the play area. Check that you cannot touch anyone or anything. This is your "Home"! Remember it. Now leave your home and touch 5 different markers, then return to "stand tall" in your home space. Go!

2. *Scrambled Eggs!* Listen carefully to how I will ask you to move. Then move in this way, in and out of each other, without "touching" anyone. "Scrambled Eggs—Walking!"

" SCRAMBLED EGGS – WALKING!"

3. *Iceberg!* This is your stopping signal. When you hear this word, stop immediately by "jump-stopping" or landing on your feet at the same time, knees bent, hands out for balance.

RUNNING   "ICEBERG!" – JUMP STOP

4. *Hit the Deck!* This is your signal to drop carefully to the ground, in front lying position. Stay there until you hear the next signal.

" HIT THE DECK! "

WARMING-UP ACTIVITIES *(Continued)*

5. ***Clear the Deck.*** Move quickly to stand *outside* on one side of the marked play area. Clear the deck again! Now move to stand *outside* another side. Continue in this way. (Vary the way children move: slide-step, skip, run high, walk low . . . .)

"CLEAR THE DECK"

6. ***Listening Line.*** (Use the boundaries of the play area.) Immediately run and stand in a long line where I am pointing. Face me and space yourself arm's length apart. Now take giant steps across to the opposite side and stand on a listening line once there. How many giant steps did you take? Return to your listening line, again counting the number of steps.

"LISTENING LINE"

7. ***Corners!*** (Use the corners of your play area.) Number the corners respectively 1, 2, 3, and 4. Have children run to one of the four corners of their choice. Give them a 10-second count to get to a corner. Draw a number out of a hat and call out that number (1, 2, 3, or 4). If the child is in the corner corresponding to the number called, then he or she must run to the middle of the play area and sit down. Continue until no one is left in a corner. Who will be the last one? *Variation:* Designate "6 corners" and use a dice. Now watch the action!

CORNER   CORNER

WARMING-UP CHALLENGES

➤ *Home.* Using your right hands, shake hands with 5 different children, then return home and shake all over like a wet dog coming out of the water.

"SHAKE HANDS"

➤ *Scrambled Eggs—Walking!* Walk forwards—watch carefully where you are going. "Iceberg!" Stretch *tall* towards the sky.

— Walk quickly; walk slowly; quickly–slowly. "Iceberg!" Stretch *wide*! "Dead Bug!"—Quickly lie on your back and wiggle your hands and feet in the air!

— Walk with big steps; walk with baby steps; walk with feet close together; walk with feet far apart. "Iceberg!"—Stork Stand! (Balance on one foot.)

— Walk happily; walk angrily; walk frightened. Creep quickly. "Iceberg!" Curl up into a ball, then slowly, very slowly uncurl and stretch tall.

— Walk in a straight line; walk in a zig-zag pattern; walk in a figure-8; walk in a circle. "Iceberg!" Touch 3 body parts to the ground.

— March to music and clap your hands in time. "Iceberg!" March in place!

"DEAD BUG!"   "BIG STEPS"   MARCH-CLAP!   "WALK"   STRETCH TALL

➤ Try a *combination of signals* and watch the action!

— "Scrambled Eggs!—Running!" "Hit the Deck!" "Clear the Deck!"

— "Scrambled Eggs!—Slide-stepping." "Iceberg!" "Hit the Deck!"

— "Scrambled Eggs!—Skipping." "Clear the Deck!"

— "Scrambled Eggs!—Leaping." "Hit the Deck!" "Pencil Stretch!"

— "Scrambled Eggs!—Hopping." "Iceberg!" "Shake–shake–shake!"

➤ Play **"Six Corners"** with several players as a challenge to see who will be the last one to get caught! When only 6 players remain, each player must run to a different corner!

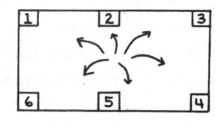

WARMING-UP GAMES

1. *Here, Where, There.* Listen carefully to the word I will say. If you hear the word "Here!" walk quickly towards me; "Where!," walk on the spot; "There," walk quickly away from me. *Variation:* Repeat this activity, having children move in other ways, such as skipping, running, jumping, slide-stepping, hopping.

2. *Follow-the-Leader.* Find a partner and stand together in a home space. Begin by facing each other about 1 meter apart. Take turns being the leader and the follower, changing on my whistle signal. Think of lots of different ways that you can move. How many different body parts can you warm up?

3. *Let's Pretend You Are.* (Remember to watch where you are going!)

   ➤ a 747 jet taking off down the runway, lifting off, and then flying

   ➤ a lawn mower cutting the grass

   ➤ a jet-ski slicing through the water

   ➤ a hawk swooping down on a small critter

   ➤ a hockey player scoring a goal

   ➤ a figure skater spinning

   ➤ a shadow-boxer punching into the air; and "dancing" with the feet

   ➤ a karate-kid, kicking with feet and slashing with hands

   ➤ a hummingbird flitting from flower to flower

   ➤ a prancing horse

   ➤ a kite dipping and lifting in the air

   ➤ a snake wriggling along the ground

STRETCHING ACTIVITIES

Stretching is one of the most important, yet most neglected fitness activities, that should be done almost every day of your life. Research has clearly indicated that children need to experience stretching activities on a daily basis. Often this is not the case. Most young children are flexible, but they quickly lose this ability if they do not stretch regularly. The benefits of stretching include an increased range of motion of joints; improved flexibility of muscles and joints; improved coordination and overall body management; prevention of injuries such as muscle strains and pulls; and development of overall body awareness.

Children with movement difficulties need to be taught to stretch from an early age, as they are more injury- and accident-prone. Teaching the young child how to fall safely or recover from a falling position has a strong carry-over value for the rest of his or her life. We have presented several different, interesting, and fun ways of getting kids to stretch and keep stretching. In fact we suggest that you do these yourself on a daily basis!

➤ *The Good Morning Stretch!*
Pretend you are still in your bed and just beginning to wake up. Lying on your back, stretch yourself as wide as possible. Do this slowly. Now stretch yourself long like a pencil. Show me how you can stretch your mouth wide open and give us a big "good morning" smile!

GOOD MORNING STRETCH!

➤ *Noddy Heads.* Stand tall. Gently and slowly nod your head as if you are saying "Yes." Now gently nod your head as if you are saying "No."

NODDY HEADS

SHOULDER SHRUGS

➤ *Shoulder Shrug.* Stand tall. Shrug your shoulders as if you are saying "I don't know." Now gently roll your shoulders backwards, then forwards.

➤ *Sky Reaches.* Stand tall. Stretch one arm up towards the sky, then stretch the other arm. Continue.

SKY REACHES

WINDMILLS

OPEN-SQUEEZE

➤ *Windmills.* Stretch your arms out sideways. Gently circle forwards. Then squeeze and open your hands.

STRETCHING ACTIVITIES *(Continued)*

➤ *Belly Button Circles.* Pretend your belly button is the center of the circle. Trace 3 circles in one direction, then 3 circles in the opposite direction. Repeat.

➤ *Knee Circles.* Stand tall with feet together. Slightly bend your knees and slowly circle knees in one direction, then circle in the opposite direction. Try to keep your upper body straight.

➤ *Side Stretcher.* Standing tall, slowly reach down one side of your body, "walking" your fingers as far down as you can go. Walk your fingers back up to starting position, and then walk your fingers down the other side.

➤ *Sunflower Stretch.* Lie on your back, arms at your sides and legs straight. Bring one leg straight upwards and gently press it towards you for 10 seconds, then repeat with the other leg.

➤ *Finger Stretcher.* In sitting position, interlock together your fingers of both hands, then gently straighten your arms pushing the palms of your fingers outwards. Hold this stretch for 5–10 seconds; relax, and repeat.

➤ *Arm Stretcher.* In cross-leg sit position, place one hand behind your back and the other hand over your shoulder. Try to make your fingers touch! Do again, reversing hand roles.

STRETCHING CHALLENGES

➤ *Angels in the Snow.* Get into back-lying position and gently spread your arms and legs wide apart, then together . . . apart . . . together . . . apart . . . together. Nicely done! Now leave your legs together and spread just your hands apart; hands by your sides and legs spread apart. Good!

ANGELS IN THE SNOW

➤ *Periscope Stretch.* Begin in back-lying position. Raise one leg and hold it in the air with opposite hand for 10 seconds. Do this again with the other leg and hand. Now hold both legs upwards for a 10-second stretch. Slowly lower and repeat.

LADYBUG STRETCH

➤ *Foot Artist.* In sitting position, lean back on hands for support. Lift one leg and draw circles in the air with your pointed toes. Now draw circles in the opposite direction. Repeat using the other foot. Use your foot to trace your favorite letter; favorite number?

FOOT ARTIST

➤ *Tense & Relax.* Suggest using soft background music with child lying on a mat or soft surface and eyes closed. Name different body parts to tighten, then relax: face, shoulders, hands, tummy, seat, legs, toes; right foot; left foot; all over!

TENSE & RELAX—HANDS

➤ *Tick-Tock.* Stand back-to-back with a partner, about half a step away from each other and interlock fingers. Bending gently at your knees, together lean to one side and touch pointer fingers to floor "tick," then lean to the other side, touching pointer fingers to floor "tock"! Continue "tick-tocks" in this way.

"TICK-TOCK"

STRENGTHENING ACTIVITIES

Good muscular strength is needed to carry out daily work and play—taking out the garbage, bringing in the groceries, chopping the wood, raking the leaves, hanging and swinging on the playground apparatus, throwing a football, swinging a baseball bat, swimming in the surf ... and even dealing with unforeseen emergencies!

Through improving the child's muscular strength, the strength of bones, ligaments, and tendons are also increased. Young children's bones are still growing and therefore need low-impact exercises or activity. The more weight-bearing activities they can experience, the better. Keeping the activities enjoyable and at the developmentally-appropriate age level will ensure proper strength development, decrease the chance of injury, prevent poor posture and back injury, and improve the child's performance.

➤ *Critter Walks.* Begin in your home space. Show me how you can move like the following "critters" (animal walks):

— *Crab Walk.* Walk on all fours face upwards.

— *Kangaroo.* Jump with hands held up in front.

— *Puppy Dog Walk.* Walk on all fours.

— *Bunny Hop.* On all fours, with hands moving forward first, then feet. Continue in this way.

— *Seal Walk.* Move along using your forearms and dragging your feet behind.

— *Inchworm Crawl.* Begin in front support position (on hands and feet, facing downwards). Walk hands away from feet, then walk feet up to hands. Continue to "inch" along in this way.

— *Bucking Bronco.* Take your weight on your hands and kick your legs gently up into the air. How high can your legs go?

Make up your own "critter walk"!

CRAB WALK

KANGAROO

PUPPY DOG WALK

BUNNY HOP

SEAL WALK

INCHWORM

BUCKING BRONCO

STRENGTHENING ACTIVITIES *(Continued)*

➤ *Bridges.* Make a bridge with your hands and feet facing downwards; facing upwards. Make a bridge on 3 body parts; 2 body parts. Make a bridge with a partner using only 3 body parts; 5 body parts.

BRIDGES

➤ *Bridges and Tunnels.* Make a bridge while your child moves through the tunnel, then reverse roles. Explore different ways.

BRIDGES & TUNNELS

➤ *Jack-in-the-Box.* Pretend you are hiding in a box. Squat down low, then spring up reaching as high as you can. Repeat.

JACK-IN-THE-BOX

➤ *Peek-a-Boos.* In hook lying position (on your back with knees bent and weight on your heels), slowly raise your head and shoulders off the floor to look at your feet, then slowly lower. Repeat.

PEEK-A-BOOS

➤ *Finger Push-Ups.* In front kneeling position, lean forward to take your weight flat on your hands, then push up on your fingers of one hand, then the other hand. Now flatten the first hand, then the second. Repeat this pattern.

FINGER PUSH-UPS

STRENGTHENING ACTIVITIES *(Continued)*

➤ *Partner Leapfrog.* One partner kneels on all fours; the other partner places hands gently on kneeling partner's back and leaps over him or her. Land and get into kneeling position, so that other partner can now leapfrog over you. Continue in this way, leapfrogging from one end of play area to other.

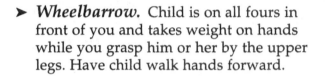

➤ *Wheelbarrow.* Child is on all fours in front of you and takes weight on hands while you grasp him or her by the upper legs. Have child walk hands forward.

➤ *Stubborn Donkey.* As for "Wheelbarrow" except that as child tries to walk hands forward, you offer resistance.

➤ *Tugs and Pushes.* Stand with partner on either side of a line. Grasp each other's right wrists and try to pull the other partner across the line. Now try again using left wrist hold. *Variation:* Stand facing partner on one foot, and gently push against the other partner's shoulder to make partner lose balance. Repeat balancing on other foot.

➤ *Climbers & Hangers.* Climb up a hanging rope. Hang on a horizontal bar. Climb and hang on the monkey bars and other playground equipment. Walk hands across the bar. What other climbing or hanging tricks can you do?

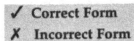

EXERCISES TO AVOID

Exercises or activities that place stress on the neck, back, knee, and other joints can be potentially harmful, especially for children who have movement difficulties and perform them incorrectly. In general, *avoid hyperextending any joint area, doing ballistic–jerky movements, or exercising unsupported areas of the body.*

Neck Area

Back Area

Knee Joint

Other

SECTION 2
BODY CONTROL SKILLS

MOTOR MEMORY

Motor memory relates to the child's ability to visually and auditorially copy single movements, movement patterns, and rhythm patterns. If a child experiences difficulties in this area, it may be appropriate to have a doctor check the child's eyesight and hearing. Start with one movement and then increase the number (one movement for each age year). The first stage is to have the child remember the moves in any order and then in the correct sequence.

MOTOR MEMORY ACTIVITIES

1. Copying hand movements: fist, palm up, palm down, hand sideways.

2. Copying touching movements to different body parts.

3. Copying body movements:
   ➤ knee up, hands on head, wiggle-wiggle
   ➤ kick-kick, punch-punch
   ➤ start low and gradually get bigger and bigger

4. Copying clapping rhythms; foot-stamping; finger-snapping.

5. Copying grid patterns. (Refer to "Grid Patterns" in this section and "Memory Jumping" in Section 3.)

6. Movement sequencing examples:
   ➤ walk on all fours—roll—jump up
   ➤ skip—slide—hop

7. Rhythm sequencing:
   ➤ 2 knee slaps, 2 hand claps, 2 finger snaps
   ➤ clap 4 times, turn around

8. Locomotion/rhythm sequencing examples:
   ➤ Walk forward 4 steps and clap, walk backwards 4 steps and clap, walk in a circle for 4 counts, then stamp-stamp-stamp-clap.
   ➤ Start from inside your hoop, hop out to the front, hop back inside; hop out to the back, hop back inside; hop out to the right and back inside; hop out to the left, back inside.

MOTOR MEMORY CHALLENGES

1. *Alphabet Arms.* On a large piece of paper write the letters of the alphabet using upper-case letters. Underneath each letter write an L, R, or B. Choose one color for the letters of the alphabet and another color for the movement letters. For an L, have child extend left arm to the side; for an R, extend right arm to side; for a B, extend both arms out in front. Have child say the letter and do the associated arm movement with that letter. Encourage child to progress at his or her own rate. Observe child's actions and the saying of the letters. Practice part by part, slowly, until child has mastered each part. Challenge child by asking him or her to do this activity backwards, or from right to left.

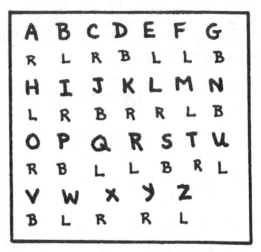

   Variations:

   ➤ Use upper case; lower case; different fonts.

   ➤ Randomly mix the letters and arm movements.

   ➤ For younger children, use shapes, pictures, and colors instead of letters.

   ➤ On the hands of young children, use colored dots instead of having them relate to the directions of left and right.

2. *Touch Memory Order.* Have child move to touch one object and then return to you to hear the next object to be touched. Now child must touch the first object, and then the second, before returning to you to hear what third object is to be touched. Child then moves to touch the first object, then the second, and then the third. Continue in this way. For example: tree—rock—door.

MOTOR MEMORY CHALLENGES *(Continued)*

3. ***The Eye Box***

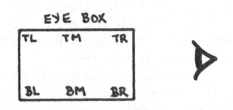

EYE BOX

> ➤ Have child draw a large rectangular box on a piece of paper. In the box mark the following locations: top right (TR), top middle (TM), top left (TL), bottom left (BL), bottom middle (BM), and bottom right (BR). Have child now point to each of these as you call them out. Do with dominant hand, then with other hand.

> ➤ Now have child stand tall and imagine that the Eye Box is in front of him or her. Call out the different locations and have child move only eyes to those places. Head must stay still. Observe his or her actions!

"TOP MIDDLE!"

> ➤ Child now marches in place and lets knees gently touch his or her hands which are held out in front.

> ➤ Do the Eye Box activity while child continues to march in place.

4. ***Movement Memory Order.*** Have child do a movement, then add on a second movement; then do movements one and two together. Now add on a third movement; then do all three movements in the correct order. Repeat with other movements. For example: blink your eyes; snap your fingers; stamp your feet. Gradually build on movements, keeping the activity appropriate to the age level of the child.

"BLINK!"

"SNAP!"

"STAMP!"

BODY IMAGE

It is essential that children have an understanding of their own body. They need to know body parts and where they are in relation to each other, as well as an internal knowledge of sidedness (that is, left and right side of the body) even though they might not be able to name them.

Eventually we would like children to be able to respond to the directional language of left and right so that they are combining their knowledge of their body with spatial concepts. It is important that children also know and can respond to the movement language associated with body image.

BODY IMAGE ACTIVITIES

1. Have child draw himself or herself, starting with one body part, then asking for one more detail each time. For example, draw your head, eyes, mouth, ears, nose, neck, body, arms, hands, fingers, and so on.

1. "EARS!"

2. On a large piece of paper, trace an outline of your child's body in back-lying position. Then have child fill in the details.

2. "EAR"

3. Have child point to the body parts you call out first with eyes open, then with eyes closed.

4. Ask questions such as: "What body part do you . . . smell with? talk with? hear with? blink with? clap with? point with? wave with? jump with?"

SKIP   5.   ELBOW

5. Simple aerobic exercises promote awareness and rhythm. Have child move to music; when music stops, child jump-stops and touches the body part you name. Vary the way the child moves.

6. Connect with child palm to palm and have child mirror-image your movements.

6. CONNECT

24

BODY IMAGE ACTIVITIES *(Continued)*

7. Ask child to move just a certain body part at a time, imitating you. "Turn your head from side to side"; "wiggle your nose"; "snap your fingers"; "open and close your mouth"; "blink your eyes."

7. "SNAP!"

8. KNEE TO TABLE

8. Now ask child to "touch a body part" to the objects in the environment: "head to ground"; "elbow to chair"; "knee to table"; and so on.

9. Now include specific directionality instructions (right and left) with body movements. Repeat the above activities adding the terms right and left. For example, shake your right hand; lift your left knee; circle your left arm; balance on your right foot.

9. CIRCLE L ARM

R ELBOW TOUCH TO L KNEE

10. Have child lie on his or her back, eyes closed. Call "lift your left arm"; "touch your right elbow to your left knee"; "hold your right foot with your left hand."

10.

11. Do different stretching exercises: raise your hands high in the air; lie on your back and stretch body parts wide; open and close your fingers.

12. Have child toss and catch a light nylon scarf on different body parts. Toss with one hand, then with the other.

11. "STRETCH"

12. SCARF ON ELBOW

13. Have child contact a balloon with different body parts: pointer finger, elbow, head, knee, foot, shoulder, nose, hand. Now try to keep the balloon in the air using only: pointer fingers and elbows; head, knee, foot; and so on.

13. Balloon contact

BODY IMAGE ACTIVITIES *(Continued)*

14. With a partner hit the balloon back and forth to each other using different body parts. How many different parts can you use?

14.

15. ***Busy Body Parts.*** (Ideally played with 4 or more children, each holding a bean-bag or similar small object.) Call out a body part; for example, "knees." Child uses beanbag to touch partner's knee. Call out another body part; for example, "elbows." Now child must find a new partner and use beanbag to touch this body part. Continue in this way.

15.   "KNEE TO KNEE"

RELATED GAMES

1. *Simon Says.* When you say "Simon Says," child responds by doing the task; when you ask child to do a task without first saying "Simon Says," child does not respond and continues to do the previous movement. How good a listener can you be? "Simon says ... wiggle your fingers." "Stamp your feet!"

" WIGGLE"

2. *Hokey Pokey*

   You put your right foot in; you put your right foot out;

   You put your right foot in and you shake it all about.

   You do the Hokey Pokey, and turn yourself around. That's what it's all about.

   Continue with left foot, right hand, left hand, head, bottom, etc.

"SHAKE LEG"

3. *If You're Happy and You Know It*

   If you're happy and you know it, clap your hands.

   If you're happy and you know it, clap your hands.

   If you're happy and you know it, then your face is gonna show it,

   If you're happy and you know it, clap your hands.

   Add other actions, such as "if you're excited and you know it, stamp your feet."

"CLAP HANDS"

SPATIAL AWARENESS

Children have to learn to cope with near (personal) and far (general) space. Otherwise many of the fundamental movement skills such as throwing, catching, and striking will be more difficult to master.

Personal space is the immediate space within reach of a child's body parts. The child who continually bumps into things or knocks objects—like the precious and highly valuable antique vase—off the table may very likely be displaying poor personal spatial skills.

The second type of spatial orientation is that of *general* space, the area in which a child (or children) and objects may move. Children who display poor evasive skills, who have difficulties in predicting the path of a ball, or judging distances, are really displaying deficiencies in general space orientation. Within the understanding of space we have knowledge of directions, such as "up and down"; levels of space, such as "high and low"; distance relationships, such as "near and far"; and temporal aspects, such as judging the speed of objects moving through space. There are also different stance positions: square, side-on, and diagonal.

SQUARE   SIDE-ON   DIAGONAL

SPATIAL ACTIVITIES

Children need to understand spatial language both verbally and physically before they can successfully move around the environment. Below are the more common terms they need to know:

near/far; beside/away; under/over; up/down; in/out; square; side on; diagonal; high/low; in front of/behind/next to; on/off; left/right; forwards/backwards/sideways; inside/outside; fast/slow; along/between; first/second/etc.; face to face/back to back; front/middle/back; close to/far away; top/bottom; round/through; opposite side; open/close; shaking; shrugging; turning; tightening (tense); stretching (extending); bending (flexing); swinging; sliding; rolling; lifting; touching; hard/soft

> **Shape Language:** circle, square, triangle, rectangle
> **Size Language:** big/bigger; small/smaller; little/large
> **Time Language:** slow/slower; fast/faster; second

1. Have child in standing tall position, feet shoulder-width apart, facing one wall of the room (or side of the play area.) Demonstrate the square, side on, and diagonal stance positions. Have child copy you, then repeat using other walls (sides) as focal points. (You could trace child's feet on paper, cut out footprints, and position in the different stance positions for child to stand on.)

SQUARE ON   SIDE-ON   DIAGONAL

1.

2. Using objects in a room, have children move to music. When the music stops, ask children to move in relation to an object or piece of equipment or another person. For example, stand *behind* something; sit *in front of* the chair; kneel *beside* the table.

"KNEEL BESIDE"

2.

3. In pairs, have one partner do one thing while other partner does the opposite. For example, one *in front of* something, the other *behind*; one *on* something, other *off*; move *over* something, other moves *under*.

"IN FRONT OF"   "BEHIND"

3.

SPATIAL ACTIVITIES *(Continued)*

4. Use beanbags or folded socks and have child place or throw object according to certain spatial commands: put beanbag on top of your head; place it behind you; put it on the side of you; in front of you; throw beanbag high.

4.

5. Have child move in spaces to your directions without touching others or furniture/objects: move between object; move around; move under; move on and off; move through.

5.

6. Have child move in spaces using different ways of traveling (locomotion): walking, sliding, hopping, skipping. Now have child move in different directions, such as walking backwards; sliding sideways; skipping forwards.

6. ----→

SKIPPING FORWARDS

7. Have child move to music in different directions, at different speeds: walking quickly backwards; skipping slowly forwards; and so on.

8. Have child move in spaces at different levels. Then think up combinations of directions, levels, locomotion, and speed: creeping medium level, slowly backwards; rolling, low, quickly sideways.

SLIDING SIDEWAYS   7.   WALKING BACKWARDS

ROLLING SIDEWAYS

8.

9. Begin to add left and right concepts to the above activities: 2 jumps forward; one hop to the left; three steps to right, pass by an object on the right; touch an object with your left foot; place beanbag on the right side of you; toss beanbag to me on my left side; bounce a ball on the right side of you; bounce in front of you; and so on.

JUMPS FORWARD   HOP L   3 STEPS R

9.

10. Repeat the above activities focusing on the different stance positions.

RELATED GAMES

1. *Ladders.* Move between the rungs using right/left concepts: move right hand, then left foot as you climb upwards, across, through, in and out of, and so on.

LADDERS

2. *Grid Patterns.* Use carpet squares or mark out a grid pattern with masking tape, then give signals for child to move. For example, start in Square 1; make 2 hops up; 3 jumps to the right; make 1 step backwards; touch your right hand to the square; beside you; put your left foot in the square in front of you; make 3 jumps diagonally downwards. Give child a directions map to follow different patterns on this grid.

SQUARE ONE

3. *Obstacle Courses.* Create an obstacle course with child; draw a map that shows how to move through the obstacle course. Move over/under; on/off; through; across; around; between; and so on.

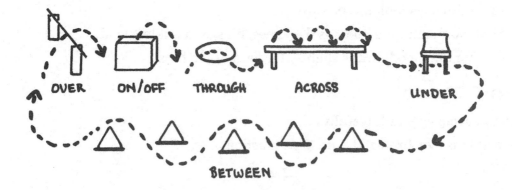

OVER   ON/OFF   THROUGH   ACROSS   UNDER   BETWEEN

JUMPS AND LANDING

JUMPING FOR DISTANCE (HORIZONTAL JUMP)

PREPARING TO MOVE

1. Head up with eyes looking forward.

2. Arms extend behind the body as the knees, hips, and ankles bend.

3. At the same time, body leans slightly forward.

MOVING

4. Legs extend vigorously and forcefully; at the same time arms extend forward and upward vigorously.

5. Jump is evenly off both feet.

6. Body remains leaning slightly forward.

TEACHABLE POINTS

1. Head up with eyes looking forward.
2. Arms extend behind the body as legs bend.
3. Legs extend forcefully.
4. Jump is evenly off both feet.
5. Arm action is strong and synchronized with the leg action.
6. Body extends upward and forward.

VERTICAL JUMPING

PREPARING TO MOVE

1. Head up with eyes looking forward.
2. Arms extend behind the body as the knees, hips, and ankles bend.
3. At the same time, body leans slightly forward at the hips.

MOVING

4. Legs and arms extend forcefully.
5. Arm action is synchronized with the leg action.

JUMPS AND LANDING *(Continued)*

6. Body extends upward.
7. Arms are extended upward.
8. Head is up and eyes are looking upward.

TEACHABLE POINTS

1. Head is up with eyes looking forward.
2. Arms extend behind the body as the legs bend.
3. Legs and arms extend forcefully at the same time.
4. Jump is evenly off both feet.

LANDINGS

TEACHABLE POINTS

1. On landing, head is up with eyes looking forward.
2. On landing, lean slightly forward at the hips.
3. Arms are held out in front or to side of body to assist balance.
4. Land on balls of both feet and then roll back onto flat feet.
5. Ankles, knees, and hips bend to absorb force.
6. Feet should be shoulder-width apart.

FALLING FORWARD AND LANDING ON HANDS

1. Contact with fingers, then palms of hands, heels of hands. Bend elbows.
2. Hands are flat, with fingers spread and slightly inward.
3. Back should be straight.
4. When contact is made, "give" by bending arms to absorb the force of the fall.

FALLING BACKWARD AND LANDING ON HANDS

1. Hands break the fall first, then the seat, back, and shoulders touch.
2. Fingers should point the same way as the toes.
3. Legs should stay high so that knees do not knock the nose.

JUMPING AND LANDING ACTIVITIES

These activities are designed to combine jumping and landing. Soft mats should be used whenever possible. Jumping activities should be combined with other movements, as too much repetition of jumps and landings can lead to muscle soreness and fatigue. Using music will add to the enjoyment of the activity and enhance rhythm.

Stand swinging the arms back and forth as the knees bend and straighten.

1. Have child jump to stand still. Ask: "How quietly can you land? Now close your eyes. Can you jump, land, and stand still?"

2. Hold the child's hand at the wrist and pull gently towards you while child attempts to jump.

3. Have child travel in different ways, jump into the air, and land.

4. Have child jump in and out of a hoop placed on the ground.

5. Have child jump in different directions: forward; backward; sideways.

6. Ask child to jump back and forth over a rope stretched out along the ground. Jump forward over the rope; backward; from side to side.

7. Have child jump as far as possible from a standing position.

8. Ask child to jump as high as possible. Have child reach for a tree branch or mark on the wall.

JUMPING AND LANDING ACTIVITIES *(Continued)*

9. Have child run into an open space. On signal "Stop" do a Jump-Stop (landing on both feet at the same time, with feet shoulder-width apart).

10. Have child jump from different heights off different apparatus.

11. Jump over different pieces of apparatus.

12. Combine jump-stopping with other movements: jump, hop, slide.

13. Jump and turn: quarter jump-turn; half jump-turn; full jump-turn. (Could use walls as focus points.) Jump-turn in one direction; jump-turn in the other.

14. Falling forward and landing: Have child kneel on a mat or suitable soft surface. Now fall forward, reaching with hands, fingers spread, to gently break the fall. Elbows bend with contact and stomach touches the mat.

15. Repeat #14 from squat position.

16. Falling backward and landing: Have child rock backwards from sitting position, arms taking the weight. From squat position, gently fall backward, letting hands break the fall; then seat, back, and shoulders touch the mat. Fingers should face same direction as toes. Child should finish with legs high so that the knees do not knock the nose.

JUMPING AND LANDING CHALLENGES

1. *Frog in the Pond.* Use a rope to create a "lily pad." Have child pretend he or she is a frog jumping up to catch a flying bug, and landing back on the lily pad. Then "frog-jump" off the lily pad and back inside the pond.

FROG IN THE POND

2. *Rabbit in the Hole.* On signal "Run rabbit run," child jumps from his or her "hole" (circled rope), runs to touch an object, then runs home to jump and land in his or her hole. Repeat, using other ways of traveling.

3. *Memory Jumping.* Use chalk to mark out a circle grid as shown. Start off with 2 instructions, then keep adding another: 2 jumps forward, 1 jump back; 2 jumps forward, 1 jump back, 3 jumps to the right; and so on.

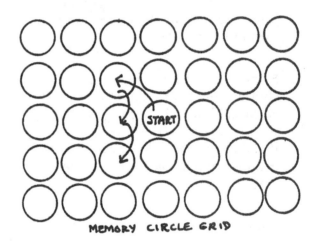

MEMORY CIRCLE GRID

4. *Dominoes.* Play with several children. Have each child in turn fall forward from squat position. Try from standing.

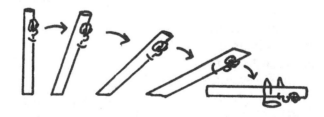

JUMPING AND LANDING CHALLENGES
(Continued)

5. ***Long Rope Jumping.*** Using a long rope with one end secured to a door knob, fence, tree, or the like, have child start in the center. Gently swing the rope around, cueing the child when to jump.

6. ***Island Jumping.*** Draw circles in any pattern you wish. Have child jump from one circle to another.

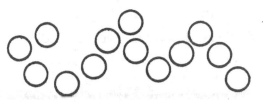

7. ***Elastic Jump.*** Use chairs and an elastic band or light cane rod. Have child jump back and forth over the elastic.

8. ***Swinging Rope Jump.*** Swing a rope gently in one circular direction just above the ground. Child must time the swing and jump over the rope! Change direction of rope and repeat. Gradually let the rope swing higher off the ground.

9. ***Hopscotch.*** Play hopscotch, which involves hopping and jumping skills. Use the hopscotch patterns presented here, then have child create his or her own.

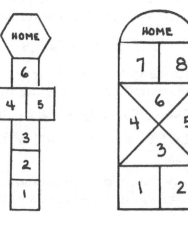

COMMON FAULTS: JUMPING

HORIZONTAL JUMPING/VERTICAL JUMPING

1. Jumping more off one foot than the other.
2. Push with the legs is not quick or strong enough.
3. Not leaning forward prior to take-off.
4. Weak arm action.
5. Arms not swung up and forward.
6. Arms not synchronized with leg action.
7. Incorrect take-off angle.
8. Head down and eyes not looking forward.

> **TEACHING TIPS: FIRST CORRECT THE COMPONENT THAT WILL HAVE THE GREATEST IMPACT.**
>
> ☞ Practical demonstration accompanied with simple and age-appropriate instruction is important when teaching children experiencing difficulties.
>
> ☞ Constant verbal and visual feedback are essential when trying to change poor movement components. This strategy is therefore applied to each and every one of these activities.
>
> ☞ Imagery can be useful in providing cues to correct movements.
>
> ☞ Motivation is essential for maintaining attention, interest, and participation.

ACTIVITIES TO CORRECT COMMON FAULTS

1. *Jumping more off one foot than the other.*

➤ Hold the feet of the child lightly and have child practice bending the knees and then straightening as child extends up onto the toes. Ask child to feel the pressure of your grip on both feet.

➤ Touch the foot that is not extending just prior to jumping and ask the child to concentrate on pushing off hard with this foot.

2. *Push with the legs is not quick or strong enough.*

➤ Include in the child's program, leg strength and abdominal exercises. (Refer to the strengthening activities in Section 1.)

➤ Observe the weight of the child and decide if weight control is necessary.

➤ Check to see if the child has the correct amount of knee bend and adjust accordingly.

➤ Have the child jump over low soft objects. Ensure that there is no chance of tripping or injury through contact.

COMMON FAULTS: JUMPING *(Continued)*

3. *Not leaning forward prior to take-off.*

➤ Have the child practice "bowing" as he or she simultaneously bends his or her knees.

➤ Gently push on the back of the head of the child as the knees bend and the arms move backwards.

4. *Weak arm action.*

➤ Have child swing the arms back and forth. Use the words "swing hard" or "big swing" to obtain the desired result.

➤ Next ask child to bend and straighten the knees with the appropriate swing of the arms. "Bend knees and swing arms back."

➤ Finally ask the child to say out loud the "arm/knee sequence."

➤ *Imagery:* Tell the child to bend the knees and put arms "right back" and, as child jumps, "reach for the cookie" (horizontally), or as far forward as possible.

➤ Introduce arm strengthening exercises if needed. (Refer to Section 1.)

5. *Arms not swung up and forward.*

➤ Have child swing the arms back and forth. Use the words "swing hard" or "big swing" to obtain the desired result.

➤ Next call the child to bend and straighten his or her knees with the appropriate swing of the arms, that is, bend the knees as the arms swing back.

➤ Finally ask the child to call the arm/knee sequence.

6. *Arms not synchronized with leg action.*

➤ Ask child to bend and straighten the knees with the appropriate swing of the arms. "Bend your knees as the arms swing back."

➤ Ask the child to call out the arm/knee sequence.

➤ *Imagery:* Tell the child to bend the knees and put arms "right back" and, as they jump, "reach for the cookie" (horizontal) or as far forward as possible.

7. *Incorrect take-off angle.*

➤ Tell child to "reach for the stars" or "stretch for the ceiling" as the child jumps upward (vertically).

➤ Tell child to "reach for the mark on the floor ahead" as the child jumps forward (horizontally) as far as possible.

8. *Head down and eyes not looking forward.*

➤ Have child focus on a point either straight ahead (horizontal jump) or upward (vertical jump).

➤ Verbally remind the child until the action is learned.

COMMON FAULTS: LANDINGS

1. Landing flat-footed, resulting in jarring.

2. Keeping feet too close together, causing over balance.

3. Keeping knees too straight, causing jarring and loss of balance.

4. Dropping head, causing rotation and loss of balance.

TEACHING TIPS: FIRST CORRECT THE COMPONENT THAT WILL HAVE THE GREATEST IMPACT.

- Practical demonstration accompanied with simple and age-appropriate instruction is important when teaching children experiencing difficulties.

- Constant verbal and visual feedback are essential when trying to change poor movement components. This strategy is therefore applied to each and every one of these activities.

- Imagery can be useful in providing cues to correct movements.

- Motivation is essential for maintaining attention, interest, and participation.

ACTIVITIES TO CORRECT COMMON FAULTS

1. Landing flat-footed, resulting in jarring.

➤ While this skill is being developed, ensure that child lands on a soft surface and the knees bend on landing.

➤ Start with small jumps and ask child to land as softly and quietly as possible. Offer suggestions as to how this can be achieved.

➤ Ask child to lean well forward as he or she lands. This will assist in the correct landing.

2. Keeping feet too close together, causing over balance.

➤ Have child stand with feet together and ask child to resist falling forward when you gently push child in the back. Now ask child to stand with feet slightly apart and repeat the procedure. Ask which position felt more balanced. Continue to widen the stance until the most stable position is obtained. This process leads to a guided discovery method of learning.

➤ Place two "foot" markers the correct width apart and well within the distance jumping capabilities of child. Ask child to land on these markers.

COMMON FAULTS: LANDINGS *(Continued)*

3. *Keeping knees too straight, causing jarring and loss of balance.*

➤ Have child stand with feet apart and legs straight and stiff. Ask child to resist falling forward when you gently push child in the back. Now ask child to stand with feet apart and knees slightly bent, and repeat the procedure. Ask which position felt more balanced. Continue to bend the knees until the most stable position is obtained. This process leads to a guided discovery method of learning.

➤ Ask child to lay on his or her back with legs up in the air and straight. Gently push the soles of his or her feet. Now ask child to bend knees slightly and, as child feels the push, to bend knees further. Ask the child which tap "jolted" less.

➤ With the previous two exercises the child will have felt the difference. Now you can verbally remind child to bend the knees on landing.

4. *Dropping head, causing rotation and loss of balance.*

➤ Have child focus straight ahead on an object before jumping and still be looking at this object after landing.

➤ Have child jump with a soft beanbag on his or her head.

HORIZONTAL JUMP

Outcome/ Appearance • Success • Consistency • Rhythm • Coordination	1. Head up with eyes looking upward.	2. Arms extend behind body as knees and ankles bend.	3. At the same time, upper body bends forward at hips.	4. Legs extend forcefully.	5. Jump is evenly off both feet.	6. Arm action is strong and synchronized with leg action.	7. Body extends upward and forward.

Equipment Required:

➤ Tape measure (optional)

➤ Chalk

➤ Masking tape

➤ Gym mat (for landing on)

Procedure (Demonstrate the process as you explain):

➤ Have child stand behind a line marked on the floor.

➤ On your signal tell child that he or she has to jump off two feet as far as possible.

➤ Allow child to pause between each effort.

➤ Mark each attempt with the chalk and encourage child to beat his or her best mark.

➤ Repeat until you have assessed all the criteria.

➤ Measuring each jump is optional, but there are some standardized test results available that you may wish to use.

Outcome/Appearance:

SCORE 3   If the jump appears synchronized, is off two feet, and vigorous. **(Achieved)**

SCORE 2   If the jump is synchronized, off two feet, but lacks vigor. **(Almost achieved)**

SCORE 1   If the jump is not synchronized and/or off two feet. **(Not yet achieved/developed)**

Assessment of Individual Criteria (Example):

6. Arm action is strong and synchronized with leg action.

SCORE 3   On this movement if the arms and legs achieve this synchronization the majority of the time. **(Achieved)**

SCORE 2   On this movement if the arms and legs achieve this synchronization but it is inconsistent. **(Almost achieved)**

SCORE 1   On this movement if the arms and legs fail to achieve this synchronization. **(Not yet achieved/developed)**

Assessment Tips:

➤ Ensure that the surface is level and firm.

➤ Encourage the child at all times, making the assessment as non-threatening as possible.

➤ Avoid distractions.

➤ Ensure the child experiences some success before ending the assessment.

➤ Make sure that the mat does not slip.

HORIZONTAL JUMP

SCORE 3: Achieved
SCORE 2: Almost achieved
SCORE 1: Not yet achieved/developed

Name	Outcome/ Appearance • Success • Consistency • Rhythm • Coordination	1. Head up with eyes looking upward.	2. Arms extend behind body as knees and ankles bend.	3. At the same time, upper body bends forward at hips.	4. Legs extend forcefully.	5. Jump is evenly off both feet.	6. Arm action is strong and synchronized with leg action.	7. Body extends upward and forward.

VERTICAL JUMP

Outcome/ Appearance • Success • Consistency • Rhythm • Coordination	1. Head up with eyes looking upward.	2. Arms extend behind body as knees and ankles bend.	3. At the same time, upper body bends for-ward at hips.	4. Legs extend force-fully.	5. Jump is evenly off both feet.	6. Arms extend upward forcefully.	7. Arm action is synchro-nized with leg action.	8. Body extends upward.

Equipment Required:

➤ Tape measure (optional)

➤ Chalk

➤ Chair (optional)

Procedure (Demonstrate the process as you explain):

➤ Have child stand side on to a wall.

➤ On your signal tell child that he or she has to jump and reach as high as possible, touching the wall with the hand closer to it at the top of the jump.

➤ Allow child to pause between each effort.

➤ Mark each attempt with the chalk and encourage child to beat his or her best mark.

➤ Repeat until you have assessed all the criteria.

➤ Measuring each jump is optional, but there are some standardized test results available that you may wish to use.

Outcome/Appearance:

SCORE 3   If the jump appears synchronized and vigorous. (Achieved)

SCORE 2   If the jump is synchronized but lacks vigor. (Almost achieved)

SCORE 1   If the jump is not synchronized. (Not yet achieved/developed)

Assessment of Individual Criteria (Example):

7. Arm action is synchronized with leg action.

SCORE 3   On this movement if the arms and legs achieve this synchronization the majority of the time. (Achieved)

SCORE 2   On this movement if the arms and legs achieve this synchronization but it is inconsistent. (Almost achieved)

SCORE 1   On this movement if the arms and legs fail to achieve this synchro-nization. (Not yet achieved/developed)

Assessment Tips:

➤ Ensure that the surface is level and firm.

➤ Encourage the child at all times, making the assessment as non-threatening as possible.

➤ Avoid distractions.

➤ Ensure the child experiences some success before ending the assessment.

➤ If the child appears to be distracted by the wall, allow the jump away from the wall.

VERTICAL JUMP

Name	Outcome/ Appearance • Success • Consistency • Rhythm • Coordination	1. Head up with eyes looking upward.	2. Arms extend behind body as knees and ankles bend.	3. At the same time, upper body bends forward at hips.	4. Legs extend forcefully.	5. Jump is evenly off both feet.	6. Arms extend upward forcefully.	7. Arm action is synchronized with leg action.	8. Body extends upward.

LANDINGS

Outcome/ Appearance • Success • Consistency • Rhythm • Coordination	1. On landing, head is up with eyes looking forward.	2. On landing, lean slightly forward at hips.	3. Arms held out in front or to side of body to assist balance.	4. Land on balls of both feet and then roll back onto flat feet.	5. Ankles, knees, and hips bend to absorb force.	6. Feet should be shoulder-width apart.

Equipment Required:

➤ Low bench or similar piece of equipment

➤ Soft flat and stable landing surface

➤ Masking tape or similar floor marker

Procedure (Demonstrate the procedure as you explain):

➤ Have child stand on a low bench approximately 18 inches (45 cm) high. Encourage the child to jump past a preset mark approximately 2 feet (60 cm) from this bench.

or

➤ Clear a space and mark a point with a cone or masking tape. Place another piece of tape approximately 18 inches (45 cm) away and ask child to jump past this mark.

➤ Allow child to pause between each effort.

➤ The child will have as many turns as is necessary for you to mark the criteria.

Outcome/Appearance:

SCORE 3   If the landing is consistently well balanced. **(Achieved)**

SCORE 2   If balance is inconsistent but evident at landings. **(Almost achieved)**

SCORE 1   If balance is rarely attained on landing. **(Not yet achieved/developed)**

Assessment of Individual Criteria (Example):

1. On landing, head is up with eyes looking forward.

SCORE 3   On this movement if the eyes and head achieve this position consistently. **(Achieved)**

SCORE 2   On this movement if the eyes and head achieve this position but it is inconsistent. **(Almost achieved)**

SCORE 1   On this movement if the eyes and head fail to achieve this position. **(Not yet achieved/developed)**

Assessment Tips:

➤ Fatigue is a factor with some young children, so allow enough time between turns to avoid tiring.

➤ Watch that the child does not attempt to jump too far; otherwise, balanced landings become difficult.

➤ Encourage the child at all times, thus making the assessment as non-threatening as possible.

➤ Avoid distractions.

➤ Ensure the child experiences some success before ending the assessment.

LANDINGS

SCORE 3: Achieved
SCORE 2: Almost achieved
SCORE 1: Not yet achieved/developed

Name	Outcome/ Appearance • Success • Consistency • Rhythm • Coordination	1. On landing, head is up with eyes looking forward.	2. On landing, lean slightly forward at hips.	3. Arms held out in front or to side of body to assist balance.	4. Land on balls of both feet and then roll back onto flat feet.	5. Ankles, knees, and hips bend to absorb force.	6. Feet should be shoulder-width apart.

STATIC BALANCE

Static balance is the ability required to maintain balance in a stationary position using different body parts as the base of support. Examples are standing on one foot or doing a handstand.

BALANCING

1. The width of the support base—whether it be the feet, knees, etc.—should decrease when less support is required and increase when more support is required.

2. Feet remain flat on the ground with the toes extended.

3. Knees are slightly flexed.

4. Hips are straight.

5. Arms may be held out away from the body to assist balance.

6. Back and shoulders are straight.

7. Head is up and body parts remain steady.

8. Eyes focus straight ahead on a fixed point.

TEACHABLE POINTS

1. Head is up and the eyes are focused straight ahead on a fixed point.

2. Feet are flat on the floor with toes extended.

3. All body parts are kept straight and still.

4. Knees are kept slightly flexed.

5. Arms can be used to assist in balancing.

STATIC BALANCING ACTIVITIES

Initially when a child is practicing balancing activities, support may be needed. Gradually reduce this support. Suggest that the child close his or her eyes and try to "feel" the position of the body and to memorize this position. Each of the balancing positions should be held for 10 seconds and repeated at least 3 times or until mastery occurs. Make sure you assist when necessary with support and demonstrate the activities in front of the child when assistance is not required. Encourage the child to balance on either foot, not just the preferred one.

1. Stand with feet together and arms out to sides.

2. Stand with feet together and hands on hips.

3. Squat with feet slightly apart and arms out to the sides. Reduce width of feet.

4. As above, with hands on hips.

5. Stand on toes with arms out to sides.

6. Stand on toes with hands on hips.

7. Stand on heels with arms out to sides.

8. Stand on heels with hands on hips.

9. Stand with one foot in front of the other; the heel of one foot touching the toe of the other and with arms out to sides; then with hands on hips. Repeat with other foot in front.

10. Stand on one foot with arms out to sides. Repeat on other foot.

11. Stand on one foot with hands on hips. Repeat on other foot.

12. Have child repeat activities 9–11 with eyes closed.

STATIC BALANCING VARIATIONS

1. Have child sit on the floor and lift legs off the floor while balancing on bottom.

2. From an all-fours position (4-point balance position), have child do a 3-point balance on hand and knee combinations.

3. As above, except have child balance on hands and feet rather than hands and knees.

4. Have child repeat activities 1–3 with eyes closed.

5. Have child practice the standing balances on a low beam of wood. (Suggest 4-inch by 2-inch, 10-cm by 5-cm, plank of wood.)

6. Have child catch objects while balancing on the beam.

7. Balance boards (commercial or home-made) or adventure playground balance apparatus are ideal pieces of equipment to further practice balances.

BALANCING CHALLENGES

1. *Bridges.* Have child explore different ways of making bridges. Use different body parts to balance on.

2. *Partner Balances.* With child, find ways of balancing on 2 body parts; 3 body parts; 4 body parts; even 5 body parts!

3. *Statues.* Have child move in different ways to music. When the music stops, have child stop and perform a balance on 1 part; on 2 parts; and so on.

5 PARTS

COMMON FAULTS: STATIC BALANCE

1. Toes curled up.

2. Too much forward or sideways leaning at the hips.

3. Poor back and shoulder posture.

4. Excessive movement in body parts.

5. Head moving and eyes looking downward.

6. Balanced position too easily given up.

7. Too slow to make adjustments or over-compensate with the adjustments.

TEACHING TIPS: FIRST CORRECT THE COMPONENT THAT WILL HAVE THE GREATEST IMPACT.

- Practical demonstration accompanied with simple and age-appropriate instruction is important when teaching children experiencing difficulties.

- Constant verbal and visual feedback are essential when trying to change poor movement components. This strategy is therefore applied to each and every one of these activities.

- Imagery can be useful in providing cues to correct movements.

- Motivation is essential for maintaining attention, interest, and participation.

ACTIVITIES TO CORRECT COMMON FAULTS

For many of these activities have the child attempt them first in a normal standing position before practicing in the balanced position.

1. *Toes curled up.*

➤ Create awareness of position of toes and tension.

➤ Make child aware of toes by alternate curling and uncurling (tightening and relaxing).

➤ Ask child to raise and lower toes off the balancing surface.

2. *Too much forward or sideways leaning at the hips.* (Use teaching aids to enhance this movement.)

➤ Balance with the hips and/or back against a wall or vertical stick.

➤ Balance with child back to back and side to side.

➤ Prevent excessive movement by lightly providing support with the hands.

COMMON FAULTS: STATIC BALANCE *(Continued)*

3. *Poor back and shoulder posture.*
(Use teaching aids to enhance this movement.)

➤ As above but concentrate on the head and shoulder blades touching the wall.

➤ Place a beanbag or similar item on the head of child to balance.

➤ When against the wall, have child stretch arms out to the side and touch the wall with the back of the hand. Ask child to maintain this position as he or she lowers arms to the sides.

4. *Excessive movement in body parts.*

➤ Provide the opportunity for the child to view him- or herself by using a full-length mirror.

➤ Copy the child moving. In this way child can obtain mirror feedback from you copying his or her movements.

➤ Have child look at a point straight ahead. Use cartoon characters as the focus point.

➤ Use sun shadows or silhouettes for child to observe his or her movements.

➤ Prevent excessive movements by placing a hand or flat stick lightly against the shoulder, hips, or both.

5. *Head moving and eyes looking downward.*

➤ Use the techniques described in common fault #4.

➤ Have child balance an object on his or her head.

6. *Balanced position too easily given up.*

➤ Motivational and constant verbal encouragement are necessary.

➤ Provide achievable short-term time targets for child.

➤ External rewards may be used initially.

7. *Too slow to make adjustments or over-compensate with the adjustments.*
(Use teaching aids to enhance this movement.)

➤ Prevent over-compensations by placing a hand or flat stick lightly against the shoulders, hips, or both.

➤ Ensure that the knees are slightly bent and have child deliberately practice raising and lowering knees and shoulders together so that he or she gets a feel for correct compensating.

STATIC BALANCE

Outcome/ Appearance • Success • Consistency • Rhythm • Coordination	1. Head is up and eyes are focused straight ahead on fixed point.	2. Feet are flat on floor with toes extended.	3. All body parts are kept straight and still.	4. Knees are kept slightly flexed.	5. Arms can be used to assist in balancing.

Equipment Required:

➤ Masking tape to mark a spot on the floor and wall

➤ Stopwatch

Procedure (Demonstrate the procedure as you explain):

➤ Clear a space where the ground is firm and level. It is a good idea to mark a spot on the ground and another on a wall at eye height for child to focus on.

➤ Have child stand on one leg with hands on hips. The hands are on the hips so that child has to rely just on balance rather than compensatory moves to assist balance.

➤ Balance should be no longer than 30 seconds, but not less than approximately 5 seconds.

➤ If child cannot balance with hands on hips, have child perform the task with hands free to assist balance. Make a note of this situation.

➤ Assess balance on both legs.

➤ Pause between attempts.

Outcome/Appearance:

SCORE 3   If balance is steady with minimal body compensations. **(Achieved)**

SCORE 2   If balance is maintained for more than the minimum time but compensations are necessary. **(Almost achieved)**

SCORE 1   If balance is not attained for the minimum time. **(Not yet achieved/developed)**

Assessment of Individual Criteria (Example):

2. Feet are flat on floor with toes extended.

SCORE 3   On this movement if the eyes and head achieve this position consistently. **(Achieved)**

SCORE 2   On this movement if the eyes and head achieve this position but it is inconsistent. **(Almost achieved)**

SCORE 1   On this movement if the eyes and head fail to achieve this position. **(Not yet achieved/developed)**

Assessment Tips:

➤ Do not ask the child to balance too long or too many times in a row on the same leg, as fatigue occurs.

➤ So that you are not assessing attentional capacity, make sure the area is free of distraction.

➤ Motivation can be a problem, so make sure you continually encourage the child to keep his or her foot off the ground.

➤ If the child lifts the leg too high or too far behind the body, show the child again how to do it. You are testing balance, not technique.

➤ Do not try to use directional terms, such as left and right foot, when assessing young children as this wastes time. Use the terms "same foot" and "other foot."

STATIC BALANCE

Name	Outcome/ Appearance • Success • Consistency • Rhythm • Coordination	1. Head is up and eyes are focused straight ahead on a fixed point.	2. Feet are flat on floor with toes extended.	3. All body parts are kept straight and still.	4. Knees are kept slightly flexed.	5. Arms can be used to assist in balancing.

DYNAMIC BALANCE

Dynamic balance is the ability to maintain balance while moving. An example is walking in a straight line on a beam.

MOVING

1. Feet are flat on the ground with toes extended.
2. Knees remain slightly bent.
3. Hips, back, and shoulders remain straight.
4. Arms are extended out to the sides for balance.
5. Head is up and upper body remains steady.
6. Eyes are focused and looking straight ahead at a fixed point.

TEACHABLE POINTS

1. Head up and eyes looking forward.
2. Back and shoulders are straight.
3. Body parts remain steady (no excessive wobble).
4. Feet are placed relatively straight along the walking path.
5. Knees are slightly flexed and the hips are straight.
6. Arms are held out away from the body to assist balance.

DYNAMIC BALANCING ACTIVITIES

The following activities are completed with the child holding arms out to the sides and in bare feet. Emphasis should be on getting a good base of support.

Start with a marked line or masking tape on the ground. Then progress to a 6-inch (15-cm) wide by 6-foot (2-m) long walking beam and gradually reduce to 4-inch width as the child becomes more competent. Support may be needed in the initial stages.

1. Have child walk forwards; walk backwards along the line with the arms out to the side.

2. Combine walking forwards and backwards with turns along the line.

3. Have child walk sideways along the line.

4. Combine these 3 types of walking.

5. Have child perform the above activities with hands on hips.

6. Have child walk heel to toe, forwards, then backwards with arms out to sides.

7. Have child walk heel to toe forwards with hands on hips. Repeat walking backwards.

8. Have child walk and step over objects of different heights. Perform first with arms out to sides; then with hands on hips.

9. Have child walk, kneel, then stand up again, with arms out to sides; with hands on hips; with arms above the head.

10. Ask child to move along the beam, changing height.

11. Ask child to move along the beam with small jumps; with jump-turn to change direction.

12. Have child catch an object (such as a beanbag) while moving along the beam.

SIDEWAYS   BACKWARDS   FORWARDS
(1-4)

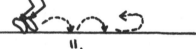

7   8.

11.

12.

DYNAMIC BALANCING VARIATIONS

For these activities apply the same teachable points as in the previous activities.

1. Have child repeat activities 1–10 while balancing an object on the head; on the hand; ball on a board.

2. Have child repeat the above activities while walking on a surface that is sloped up and down; sideways.

3. Have child walk on surfaces that are not flat, such as small dome markers.

4. Set up obstacle courses or balance stations incorporating different challenges.

5. *Object Balancing.* Have child walk along these surfaces while balancing an object on the head; on the hand; while holding a ball on a small board.

6. Have child bounce a ball to the side of the beam while walking along the beam.

RELATED GAMES

For the following activities, a marked court is ideal:

➤ *Stork Stance Tag.* Have child run/walk along the lines while you or a partner give chase. Runner is in a safe position whenever in a "stork stance"; chaser must count to 3, then again give chase. If runner is tagged, then roles are exchanged.

➤ *Turtle Tag.* Played as above, except safe position is on the back, holding limbs.

➤ *Inchworm Tag.* Safe position is on all fours, with seat raised to highest part.

STORK STANCE TAG

STORK STANCE

INCHWORM TAG

TURTLE TAG

COMMON FAULTS: DYNAMIC BALANCE

1. Toes curled up.

2. Too much forward or sideways leaning at the hips.

3. Excessive movement in body parts.

4. Poor back and shoulder posture.

5. Head moving and eyes looking downward.

6. Balanced position too easily given up.

7. Too slow to make adjustments or over-compensate with the adjustments.

TEACHING TIPS: FIRST CORRECT THE COMPONENT THAT WILL HAVE THE GREATEST IMPACT.

☞ Practical demonstration accompanied with simple and age-appropriate instruction is important when teaching children experiencing difficulties.

☞ Constant verbal and visual feedback are essential when trying to change poor movement components. This strategy is therefore applied to each and every one of these activities.

☞ Imagery can be useful in providing cues to correct movements.

☞ Motivation is essential for maintaining attention, interest, and participation.

ACTIVITIES TO CORRECT COMMON FAULTS

1. Toes curled up.
(Create awareness of position of toes and tension.)

➤ Make child aware of toes by alternate curling and uncurling (tightening and relaxing).

➤ Ask the child to raise and lower toes off the balancing surface.

2. Too much forward or sideways leaning at the hips.
(Use teaching aids to enhance this movement.)

➤ Balance with the hips and/or back against a wall or vertical stick.

➤ Balance with child back to back and side to side.

➤ Prevent excessive movement by lightly providing support with the hands.

3. Excessive movement in body parts.

➤ Provide the opportunity for the child to view him- or herself by using a full-length mirror.

➤ Copy the child moving. In this way child can obtain mirror feedback from you copying his or her movements.

COMMON FAULTS: DYNAMIC BALANCE
(Continued)

➤ Have child look at a point straight ahead. Use cartoon characters as the focus point.

➤ Use sun shadows or silhouettes for child to observe his or her movements.

➤ Prevent excessive movements by placing a hand or flat stick lightly against the shoulder, hips, or both.

4. *Poor back and shoulder posture.*
(Use teaching aids to enhance this movement.)

➤ As #2 but concentrate on the head and shoulder blades touching the wall.

➤ Place a beanbag or similar item on the head of the child to balance.

➤ When against the wall have child stretch his or her arms out to the side and touch the wall with the back of the hand. Ask the child to maintain this position as he or she lowers arms to the sides.

5. *Head moving and eyes looking downward.*

➤ Provide the opportunity for the child to view him- or herself by using a full-length mirror.

➤ Copy the child moving. In this way child can obtain mirror feedback from you copying his or her movements.

➤ Have child look at a point straight ahead. Use cartoon characters as the focus point.

➤ Use sun shadows or silhouettes for child to observe his or her movements.

➤ Prevent excessive movements by placing a hand or flat stick lightly against the shoulder, hips, or both.

➤ Have child balance a beanbag on his or her head.

6. *Balanced position too easily given up.*

➤ Motivational and constant verbal encouragement are necessary.

➤ Provide achievable short-term time targets for child.

➤ External rewards may be used initially.

7. *Too slow to make adjustments or over-compensate with the adjustments.*
(Use teaching aids to enhance this movement.)

➤ Prevent over-compensations by placing a hand or flat stick lightly against the shoulders, hips, or both.

➤ Ensure that the knees are slightly bent and have child deliberately practice raising and lowering knees and shoulders together so that he or she gets a feel for correct compensation.

DYNAMIC BALANCE

Outcome/ Appearance • Success • Consistency • Rhythm • Coordination	1. Head up and eyes looking for-ward.	2. Back and shoulders straight.	3. Body parts remain steady (no excessive wobble).	4. Feet placed relatively straight along walking path.	5. Knees slightly flexed and hips straight.	6. Arms held out away from body to assist bal-ance.

Equipment Required:

➤ Masking tape

Procedure (Demonstrate the procedure as you explain):

➤ Clear a space and place on firm and level ground. Place a piece of masking tape approximately 10 feet (3 meters) long on the floor and ask child to walk heel to toe along this masking tape.

➤ Thank child for his or her effort.

➤ Allow child to pause between efforts.

➤ The child will have as many turns as is necessary for you to mark the criteria.

Outcome/Appearance:

SCORE 3   If feet are consistently placed on the line heel to toe and balance is maintained. (Achieved)

SCORE 2   If deviation from the line and some imbalances occur. (Almost achieved)

SCORE 1   If difficulty maintaining balance and staying on the line. (Not yet achieved/developed)

Assessment of Individual Criteria (Example):

2. Back and shoulders straight.

SCORE 3   On this movement if the back and shoulders achieve this position consistently. (Achieved)

SCORE 2   On this movement if the back and shoulders achieve this position but it is inconsistent. (Almost achieved)

SCORE 1   On this movement if the back and shoulders fail to achieve this position. (Not yet achieved/developed)

Assessment Tips:

➤ Don't let the child place a gap between the heel and the toe.

➤ Make sure there are no distractions while the child is completing the movement.

➤ Encourage the child at all times, making the assessment as non-threatening as possible.

➤ Avoid distractions.

➤ Ensure the child experiences some success before ending the assessment.

DYNAMIC BALANCE

Name	Outcome/ Appearance • Success • Consistency • Rhythm • Coordination	1. Head up and eyes looking forward.	2. Back and shoulders straight.	3. Body parts remain steady (no excessive wobble).	4. Feet placed relatively straight along walking path.	5. Knees slightly flexed and hips straight.	6. Arms held out away from body to assist balance.

SECTION 3

LOCOMOTION SKILLS

WALKING

MOVING

1. Feet alternately contact ground with heel, then toe.

2. Feet are placed in a straight line on the ground.

3. Legs move in a straight line, feet slightly toed out.

4. A slight forward lean of the body.

5. Arms are slightly bent 90° at the elbow and move in opposition to the legs (when one leg is forward, the opposite arm is forward).

6. Arms move back and forth in a straight line.

7. Hands are held in relaxed position (as if holding an egg in each).

8. Head and upper body are stable and the eyes are looking forward.

9. Action looks rhythmical and smooth.

TEACHABLE POINTS

1. Head up and eyes looking in the direction of walking.

2. Body and limbs move in a straight line in the direction of the movement.

3. Feet are straight when in contact with the ground (not turned in or out).

4. Arms are slightly bent at the elbow and work in opposition to legs.

5. Hands are relaxed.

6. Arms drive actively in opposition to the swinging leg.

7. Child lands on the heel, then moves up onto the toes.

WALKING ACTIVITIES

Use marked courts that are available as the lines provide visual guidelines for the children. Using music helps establish a sense of rhythm. Equipment such as string or markers (ice cream containers) placed on the ground could be used. Some of these activities are best done at the local park. Back and hamstring flexibility exercises should be practiced regularly.

1. Place 10-m length of string on the ground and have child walk along the string, keeping it in the middle of his or her stance with feet parallel to the string. Make sure child is relaxed and his or her toes point forward. First allow child to look at his or her feet, then complete without looking. Slowly increase the speed of the movement.

2. Have child walk on the spot with knees touching his or her hands, which are held in front at waist height. Tell child to keep relaxed with head held up and looking forward. Repeat walking along the string or line slowly increasing the speed.

3. Have child march in different directions with knees lifting and arm swinging. Be a happy "marcher"! Use marching music.

4. Walk along the lines of a basketball court. Start slowly, get faster and faster. Use your arms to help you walk faster. Now you are power walking!

5. Imagine you are holding an egg in each hand as you swing your arms back and straight ahead. Hold a beanbag in each hand and walk in a straight line. Walk in a circle. Walk in a square. Walk in a figure-8. Are you using your arms to help you walk?

WALKING ACTIVITIES *(Continued)*

6. Walk taking giant steps; baby steps. Walk with feet close together; feet apart.

7. Walk on your tiptoes—walk tall. Walk low. Walk on your heels. Walk fast; walk slow; fast—slow. Stamp your feet as you walk along.

8. Walk with a beanbag on your head. If it falls off, carefully bend down to pick it up and place it back on your head.

9. Walk backwards along a line. Keep watching where you are going!

10. Now walk 3 steps forward, then walk in another direction. Continue to walk this pattern. Try this walking backwards.

11. Walk in and out of the markers. Return by walking backwards in and out of the markers.

12. Listen to my music. Can you clap the rhythm? Now let's go walking to the music. Let's create a "walking dance"—four steps forward, four steps backward, four steps in place.

13. Be a happy walker; excited walker; sad walker; frightened walker; angry walker; lazy walker. Let me guess how you are feeling by the way you walk.

14. *Follow-the-Leader:* Partners take turns being the leader. Walk in different ways and directions.

RELATED GAMES

1. *Touching Game.* Child walks forward or backward to "touch" various objects that you call out, such as a swing, a tree, a ball. Combine 2 or 3 tasks together such as: walk forward to touch 2 trees; then backwards to touch the fence; sideways to touch the red line.

2. *Walking Tag Game.* Tagger holds a beanbag in hand to use as tagging object. A tagged player must march in place until signal to stop is given. A new tagger is chosen and tag game begins again.

3. *Line Tag.* Played the same as for walking tag, except players are only allowed to move on the lines of the floor.

4. *Cars.* Children pretend they are cars. On your signal "green light," they walk forward; on signal "red light," they jump-stop; on signal "yellow light," they march in place.

5. *Can You Walk Like . . .* Find your own home space. Show me how you can walk like a penguin; a crab; a gorilla; a robot; an elephant. Invent your own animal walk!

WALKING IDEAS

1. *Walk-About.* Go walking with your child in the neighborhood, through a local park, along the beach, on the school playground. Walk at a good tempo and have a great visit with each other! Take the dog along, too!

2. *Walk-er-cise.* On a rainy or cold wintry day, put on your favorite "walking" music and walk in place or in a suitable part of your house. Pretend as you walk that you are going to the beach. Keep your feet walking as your arms do the front crawl; the breaststroke; the backstroke; the dog paddle. Walk in time to the music. March in time to the music.

FRONT CRAWL   BREAST STROKE   WALKING MUSIC

3. *Water-Walking Ideas*

   ➤ Have child hold a kick-board and walk across the pool.

   ➤ Face each other across the pool, and exchange places by walking. Who can get to the other side first?

   ➤ Hold child's hands and walk in a circle in one direction, then change directions.

   ➤ Walk in knee-deep water in the ocean on a sunny day when the waves are calm.

COMMON FAULTS: WALKING

1. Steps taken are too short.

2. Feet turned too far outwards.

3. Walking on toes instead of heel–toe movement.

4. Landing too heavily.

5. Arms not moving in opposition to the legs.

6. Hands clenched in a fist creating too much tension.

7. Head moving and eyes not facing forward.

8. Jerky walking action.

> **TEACHING TIPS: FIRST CORRECT THE COMPONENT THAT WILL HAVE THE GREATEST IMPACT.**
>
> ☛ Practical demonstration accompanied with simple and age-appropriate instruction is important when teaching children experiencing difficulties.
>
> ☛ Constant verbal and visual feedback are essential when trying to change poor movement components. This strategy is therefore applied to each and every one of these activities.
>
> ☛ Imagery can be useful in providing cues to correct movements.
>
> ☛ Motivation is essential for maintaining attention, interest, and participation.

ACTIVITIES TO CORRECT COMMON FAULTS

1. Steps taken are too short.

➤ Place markers at regular intervals and have child walk from marker to marker.

➤ Have child march to increase knee lift and stride length.

➤ Teach child to relax while walking.

➤ *Imagery:* Ask child to pretend he or she is a giant taking large steps.

2. Feet turned too far outwards.

➤ Have child practice line walking.

➤ *Imagery:* Have child imagine that his or her feet are pointing in the opposite direction to what they normally do.

3. Walking on toes instead of heel–toe movement.

➤ Have child walk a line, verbally instructing child to place the heel down first with each stride.

COMMON FAULTS: WALKING *(Continued)*

➤ Have child call out the heel placement as he or she walks heel–toe: "heel–toe! heel–toe!"; and so on.

4. *Landing too heavily.*

➤ Have child concentrate on bending the knees on landing.

➤ *Imagery:* Have child pretend he or she is walking across shells or something similar that must not break!

➤ *Imagery:* Have child walk as quietly as possible without tiptoeing.

5. *Arms not moving in opposition to the legs.*

➤ Start by having child stand with feet together and arms at sides. Take one of the child's arms and move it forward. Then have child move the opposite foot forward. Take the other arm and move it forward and have child move the opposite foot forward. Now let child—in slow motion—move opposite arm and foot forward as he or she walks in a forward direction. Gradually have child speed up the arm and foot movements.

➤ Have child march to music in place, and then move forward.

6. *Hands clenched in a fist creating too much tension.*

➤ Have child do arms and shoulders flexibility exercises. (Refer to stretching activities in Section 1.)

➤ *Imagery:* Have child imagine he or she is holding an egg in each hand and must not crush it!

7. *Head moving and eyes not facing forward.*

➤ Have child focus on a target while walking.

➤ Have child walk with a beanbag on the head.

➤ Place a mark on your back on which the child has to focus and play Follow the Leader. Apart from just walking, you can include or even start with other forms of locomotion.

➤ Verbally remind child to keep looking forward.

8. *Jerky walking action.*

➤ Have child walk to a beat (hand-clap or drum beat); start slowly and build up the pace gradually.

➤ Have child walk to music. Start with walking (marching) on the spot and slowly increase pace.

WALKING

Outcome/ Appearance • Success • Consistency • Rhythm • Coordination	1. Head up and eyes looking in direction of walking.	2. Body and limbs move in straight line in direction of movement.	3. Feet straight when in contact with ground (not turned in or out).	4. Arms slightly bent at elbow and work in opposition to legs.	5. Hands are relaxed.	6. Arms move actively in opposition to swinging leg.	7. Lands on heel, then moves up onto toes.

Equipment Required:

> 2 marker cones

Procedure (Demonstrate the procedure as you explain):

> Ask child to walk normally from one cone to the other.
> Observe the action from the side and front.
> Allow child to pause between efforts.
> Repeat until you have assessed all the criteria.

Outcome/Appearance:

SCORE 3   If the action appears correct, rhythmical, and relaxed. **(Achieved)**

SCORE 2   If the action appears rhythmical and mostly correct. **(Almost achieved)**

SCORE 1   If the action is jerky and a number of actions appear incorrect. **(Not yet achieved/developed)**

Assessment of Individual Criteria (Example):

3. Feet straight when in contact with ground (not turned in or out).

SCORE 3   On this movement if the feet achieve this straight position the majority of the time. **(Achieved)**

SCORE 2   On this movement if the feet are slightly turned in or out. **(Almost achieved)**

SCORE 1   On this movement if the feet are excessively turned in or out. **Not yet achieved/developed)**

Assessment Tips:

> Encourage the child at all times, making the assessment as non-threatening as possible.
> Avoid distractions.
> Avoid assessment if it is too windy and never walk the children into or across the wind.
> Ensure the surface is firm and even.
> You may want to walk the child along a line to assess the positioning of the feet.

WALKING

Name	Outcome/ Appearance • Success • Consistency • Rhythm • Coordination	1. Head up and eyes looking in direction of walking.	2. Body and limbs move in straight line in direction of movement.	3. Feet straight when in contact with ground (not turned in or out).	4. Arms slightly bent at elbow and work in opposition to legs.	5. Hands are relaxed.	6. Arms move in opposition to swinging leg.	7. Lands on heel, then moves up onto toes.

RUNNING

MOVING

1. Both feet are off the ground for a brief time.
2. Feet are placed in a straight line on the ground.
3. Legs move in a straight line.
4. For sprint running the supporting leg lands on the forefoot.
5. Non-support leg is flexed close to the buttocks (at least 90°).
6. Knee lift is at right angles at the front of the movement.
7. A slight forward lean of the body.
8. Arms are bent approximately 90° at the elbow, and drive actively in opposition to the legs (when one leg is forward, the opposite arm is forward).
9. Hands held in a relaxed position as if holding an egg in each one.
10. Arms move back and forth in a straight line.
11. Head and upper body are stable and the eyes are looking forward.
12. Action looks rhythmical and smooth.

TEACHABLE POINTS

1. Head remains up, with eyes looking forward in the direction of the movement.
2. Feet and legs move in a straight line in the direction of movement.
3. Arms are bent approximately 90° at the elbow.
4. Arms drive actively in opposition to the legs.
5. Knee lift is close to right angles during the recovery phase.
6. Both feet are off the ground for a brief time.
7. Body is leaning slightly forward.
8. For sprint running, the supporting leg lands on the forefoot.

74

RUNNING ACTIVITIES

Equipment includes string or markers (such as ice cream containers) placed on the ground. Some of these activities are best done at the local park. Marked courts are useful, as the lines provide visual guidelines for the children. Using music helps establish a sense of rhythm. Back and hamstring flexibility exercises should be practiced regularly.

1. Place 10-m length of string on the ground and have child run along the string, keeping it in the middle of his or her stance with feet parallel to the string Make sure child is relaxed and his or her toes point forward. First allow child to look at his or her feet, then complete without looking. Slowly increase the speed of the movement.

2. Have child jog on the spot with knees touching his or her hands, which are held in front at waist height. Tell child to keep relaxed with head held up and looking forwards. Repeat jogging along the string or line slowly increasing the speed.

3. Have child relax hands pretending to hold an egg in each hand. Moving feet in place, have child move his or her hands back and straight forward. Now have child jog along a line. Observe child's hand position and offer praise for good performance.

4. Have child hold an object, such as a beanbag, can of soup, or small weights, in each hand. Observe hand/arm movements as child jogs along a line.

5. Have child copy you running in slow motion in a straight line along the string, completing the knee lift; use correct arm action and leg lift behind the body. Emphasize head up and looking forwards.

1.

2.

4.

5. "SLOW MOTION"

RUNNING ACTIVITIES *(Continued)*

6. As child masters this, slowly build the speed, making sure that the action is completed along a line or piece of string on the ground or between two lines. As the speed increases, so should the emphasis on starting to lean slightly forward, and landing on the forefoot. Have the child change to different paces at your call.

6.

7. Try stair running to increase knee lift if required.

7.

8. To increase stride length, place 10 markers at even intervals and have child place a foot at each marker while running. Gradually increase the distance between the markers. (Do not increase the distance to the point where the action looks uncomfortable.)

9. Using markers have the child practice bounding exercises, springing from one foot to the next.

9.

10. When child is becoming competent, place markers on the ground about 2 m apart and have child zig-zag between to improve agility.

11. Have child lie on his or her front or back. On your signal, child must quickly stand up and run to a designated point. Repeat using other starting positions: cross-leg sitting; standing backwards.

11.

12. Play music with a steady strong 4/4 tempo. Have child jog in time to the music. Observe running style and provide comment.

12.

RELATED GAMES

1. ***North, South, East, West.*** Child runs in the direction you point and call out. On signal "Freeze!" child jump-stops and remains motionless, waiting for your next direction signal.

2. ***Touch 'n Go.*** Child runs to "touch" various objects that you call out, such as a tree, a swing, a fence, and so on. Put 2 or 3 directions together, such as: run forward to touch the fence with (right) knee; jog backward to touch tree with your backside; run forward to touch swing with your (left) elbow.

3. ***Beanbag Tag.*** Have child pair up with you or another child. On "Go" signal, child gives chase trying to tag you with the beanbag. If child succeeds, you become the tagger. Continue in this way.

4. ***Running Signals.*** On your signal, call out a certain way of running (explain briefly and demonstrate), then have child perform the movement:

   ➤ Jog on the spot.

   ➤ Run on your toes.

   ➤ Run stiffly like a wooden man.

   ➤ Run while clapping hands; snapping fingers; change direction every 4 claps.

   ➤ Run, letting your heels touch your back side.

   ➤ Run in place, drop to the ground, stand up, and continue to run.

RUNNING IDEAS

STAIR-CLIMBING

VARIATION

1. ***Run-About.*** Take child for a jog along the beach, through the park, on the school playground, in the neighborhood around the block. Run, then walk, then run as required.

2. ***Jog-Er-Cise.*** On a rainy or cold wintry day when you cannot be out- side, play music with a steady 4/4 beat and jog together in a suitable play area. Add arm movements such as reaching upwards, opening and closing arms sideways; swimming strokes. Go stair-climbing if steps are available to use!

3. ***This Way, That Way!*** Place 2 obstacles (chairs, hoops, markers) about 10 m (20 feet) apart. Have chil- dren pair off. First pair stand in mid- dle between the two markers, each in his or her own home space as shown. On your signal "Go!" one partner goes one way towards mark- er ("this way"); other partner goes the opposite way ("that way") towards the other marker. The chal- lenge is to see which partner can run around the marker and return to home space more quickly! *Variations:*

   ➤ Place beanbags (or a similar object) on opposite lines spaced 10 m (20 feet) apart and repeat the above challenge.

   ➤ Gradually increase the running distance.

COMMON FAULTS: RUNNING

1. Poor drive and push off the forefoot.

2. Length of the step is too small.

3. Legs and arms not moving straight forward, but outward, or across the body, causing too much upper body movement.

4. Flat-footed running.

5. The foot being placed on the ground with the toes pointing outward.

6. Non-support leg does not flex sufficiently toward the buttock; therefore, the knee lift becomes too low.

7. Trunk too upright or too far forward.

8. The arms are not flexed enough (less than 90° at the elbows).

9. Arms not moving in opposition to the legs.

10. Head moving and the eyes not facing forward.

TEACHING TIPS: FIRST CORRECT THE COMPONENT THAT WILL HAVE THE GREATEST IMPACT.

☛ Practical demonstration accompanied with simple and age-appropriate instruction is important when teaching children experiencing difficulties.

☛ Constant verbal and visual feedback are essential when trying to change poor movement components. This strategy is therefore applied to each and every one of these activities.

☛ Imagery can be useful in providing cues to correct movements.

☛ Motivation is essential for maintaining attention, interest, and participation.

ACTIVITIES TO CORRECT COMMON FAULTS

1. Poor drive and push off the forefoot.
(Need to improve leg and abdominal strength.)

➤ Incorporate leg strength exercises into child's program. (Refer to strengthening activities in Section 1.)

➤ Set up bounding exercises from marker to marker (hoop to hoop) where the knee lift and flight are exaggerated.

2. Length of the step is too small.

➤ Place markers and have child stride to each one. Gradually increase the distance between the markers.

COMMON FAULTS: RUNNING (Continued)

➤ Set up bounding exercises where the knee lift and flight are exaggerated.

➤ *Imagery:* Ask child to imagine his or her legs are springs that bounce the body forward each time the foot hits the ground. Cue word is "Spring."

3. **Legs and arms not moving straight forward, but outward, or across the body, causing too much upper body movement.**

   ➤ Take child's arms and move them alternately back and forth. Have child march like a soldier.

   ➤ *Imagery:* Ask child to imagine his or her arms are moving straight forward from the body. Start slowly and move over small distances.

4. **Flat-footed running or the foot being placed on the ground with the toes pointing outward.**

   ➤ Have child walk and then run along lines.

   ➤ Have child exaggeratedly jog on the toes.

5. **Non-support leg does not flex sufficiently toward the buttock; therefore, the knee lift becomes too low.**

   ➤ Introduce hamstring and lower back flexibility exercises into child's program. (Refer to stretching activities in Section 1.)

   ➤ Have child run up stairs to increase knee lift.

   ➤ Have child march like a soldier.

6. **Trunk too upright or too far forward.**

   ➤ Have child run up or down a slight incline and ask child to concentrate on how his or her body feels. See if child can reproduce the feeling on flat surface.

   ➤ *Imagery:* Ask child to imagine that he or she has a string attached to his or her chest or back and he or she is being pulled forward or backward.

7. **The arms are not flexed enough (less than 90° at the elbows).**

   ➤ Have child pretend he or she is marching.

   ➤ At slower paces have child balance a ribbon or soft beanbag on his or her forearm.

COMMON FAULTS: RUNNING *(Continued)*

8. *Arms not moving in opposition to the legs.*

➤ Start by having child stand with feet together and arms at sides. Take one of child's arms and move it forward. Then have child move the opposite foot forward. Take the other arm and move it forward and have child move the opposite foot forward. Now let child—in slow motion—move opposite arm and foot forward as he or she walks in a forward direction. Gradually have child speed up the arm and foot movements.

➤ Have child march in place to music, and then move forward.

9. *Head moving and the eyes not facing forward.*

➤ Have child focus on a target while running.

➤ Have child jog with a beanbag on head.

➤ Place a mark on your back on which child has to stay focused, and play Follow the Leader. Apart from just running, include other forms of locomotion.

➤ Verbally remind child to keep looking forward.

RUNNING

Outcome/ Appearance • Success • Consistency • Rhythm • Coordination	1. Head remains up, with eyes looking forward in direction of movement.	2. Feet and legs move in straight line in direction of movement.	3. Arms bent 90° at elbow.	4. Arms drive actively in opposition to legs.	5. Knee lift is close to right angles during recovery phase.	6. Both feet off ground for brief time.	7. Body leans slightly forward.	8. For sprint running, supporting leg lands on the forefoot.

Equipment Required:

➤ 2 cones

➤ Stopwatch (optional)

➤ Lane lines or similar line markings child runs along (optional)

Procedure (Demonstrate the procedure as you explain):

➤ Place 2 cones 15–20 yards/meters apart on the marked lines.

➤ Ask child to run as fast as possible along the line from one marker to the next and then slowly walk back to the first marker.

➤ For the first few trials, position yourself to the side of child. For the remainder of the trials, position yourself in front of child especially to assess criteria #2.

➤ A stopwatch may be used to gather times, as there are standardized scores available for running.

Outcome/Appearance:

SCORE 3   If the run appears well coordinated and speed is adeqaute. **(Achieved)**

SCORE 2   If the run appears reasonably coordinated; may have some incorrect movements but speed still appears to be adequate. **(Almost achieved)**

SCORE 1   If the run lacks coordination and speed. **(Not yet achieved/developed)**

Assessment of Individual Criteria (Example):

3. Arms bent 90° at elbow.

SCORE 3   On this movement if the arms achieve this position consistently. **(Achieved)**

SCORE 2   On this movement if the arms achieve this position but it is inconsistent. **(Almost achieved)**

SCORE 1   On this movement if the arms fail to achieve this position. **(Not yet achieved/developed)**

Assessment Tips:

➤ Be aware that speed will be affected by fitness, flexibility, and body weight as well as technique.

➤ Encourage the child at all times, making the assessment as non-threatening as possible.

➤ Avoid distractions.

➤ Avoid running assessment if it is too windy. Never run the children into or across the wind.

➤ If assessing a group, have each child complete 4 runs and then rest while the remainder of the group have their turn. If necessary, repeat the cycle.

➤ Ensure the surface is firm and even.

RUNNING

SCORE 3: Achieved
SCORE 2: Almost achieved
SCORE 1: Not yet achieved/developed

Name	Outcome/ Appearance • Success • Consistency • Rhythm • Coordination	1. Head remains up, with eyes looking forward in direction of movement.	2. Feet and legs move in straight line in direction of movement.	3. Arms bent 90° at elbow.	4. Arms drive actively in opposition to legs.	5. Knee lift is close to right angles during recovery phase.	6. Both feet off ground for brief time.	7. Body leans slightly forward.	8. For sprint running, supporting leg lands on forefoot.

DODGING

Dodging is a running movement with quick changes of direction. It is an essential skill for many sports such as football, ice hockey, soccer, basketball, and tennis. Dodging requires good spatial awareness and body management.

MOVING

1. Head remains up and steady.
2. Eyes stay focused in direction of travel throughout the dodge.
3. Direction is changed by pushing off outside of foot.
4. Push off is forceful.
5. Body is lowered during change of direction by bending at the knee.
6. Change of direction created in one step.
7. Knee of the supporting leg is bent as the direction change occurs.
8. Movement is from right to left; left to right; and so on.
9. Balance is maintained.

TEACHABLE POINTS

1. Head is up and the eyes are focused straight ahead in the direction of the movement.
2. Change of direction is initiated by pushing off with the outside of the foot.
3. Knee of the supporting leg is bent as the direction change occurs.
4. Body is lowered during the direction change.
5. Change of direction occurs quickly in one step.

DODGING ACTIVITIES

Equipment includes markers such as cones, witch's hats, or ice cream containers placed on the ground. Marked courts are useful, as lines provide visual guidelines. Children should be sufficiently warmed up before any dodging activities commence. See Section 1 for suggested warming-up activities for large muscle groups.

1. Have child walk in general space. On signal "whistle blast" or your signal "dodge," child makes a quick change of direction.

1-2.

2. Repeat activity 1, having child jog in general space.

3. Place a marker on the ground. Have child walk up to marker, then make a quick change of direction to either the right or the left of the marker.

3.

4. Repeat this activity, but call "right" or "left" to signal that child dodges in that direction. Now have child run up to marker and quickly change direction to right or left of marker.

5. Repeat activity 4, but signal "right" or "left" for child to dodge in that direction.

5.

6. Set up several cone markers in a straight line, spaced about 3 m apart. Have child "weave" in and out of the cone markers while walking.

7. Repeat activity 6, but have child jog.

6.

8. Now have child dodge as quickly as possible in and out of the markers.

9. Set the cone markers 2 m apart and repeat activities 6, 7, and 8.

9.

RELATED GAMES

Demonstrate in these games that by practicing the correct technique, the child won't get caught so often, or can catch you more often.

1. *Artful Dodger.* Find a partner and stand one behind the other. On the "go" signal or when the music starts, the front partner—"the dodger"—walks in general space, making quick changes of direction. The other partner is the "shadow" and tries to follow as closely as possible to the dodger without touching him or her. On the "whistle blast" both partners come to a jump-stop and freeze. If the shadow can take one step forward and touch the dodger, then the two partners change roles. Continue in this way. Use other locomotor movements such as running, slide stepping, and skipping.

RUNNING

SKIPPING

SLIDE-STEPPING

2. *Chasey.* Simple tag games provide good opportunities for children to practice their dodging skill. Mark off a large play area for the chasey games and emphasize that children must stay inside the boundaries. Gradually decrease the area. Remind children to remember to watch where they are going at all times! Now try the following ideas for creating several types of tag activities.

3. *Beanbag Tag.* Everyone holds a beanbag in the hand and uses it to tag each other. If tagged, beanbag must go on tagged player's head and tagged player jogs on the spot. On your signal "Free" everyone is freed, and the game begins again. Have children move in different ways: walking, running, slide-stepping, skipping. Use other objects as the tagging object such as small soft balls and rubber rings.

RELATED GAMES *(Continued)*

4. *Heads and Tails.* Use signal "Listening Line" and have children quickly move to stand on the line, facing you, and equally spacing themselves arms-length apart. Children alternatively label themselves "Head" or "Tail." If a "Head," child places one hand on top of head; if a "Tail," child places one hand on backside. On your Signal, "Heads or Tails," children use free hand to tag an opposite player: "Heads" will tag "Tails," "Tails" will tag "Heads" and if tagged, you are transformed into the same mode as the player who tagged you. Continue in this way. On "Iceberg" everyone stops immediately. Count the number of "Heads" and "Tails." *Variation:* Play again but this time add "Pockets" with one-third of the players having one hand in a pocket.

5. *Tail Snatch.* Use 3-inch by 12-inch non-fraying strips of cloth (8 cm × 30 cm) and have children tuck their "tail" in the back of their shorts. On signal "Snatch," each player tries to snatch the others' tails. Once a player has grabbed a tail, it stays in his or her hand, and the player uses the free hand to grab other tails. Even if a player is "tail-less," continue to play the game until everyone has lost his or her original tail. *Variation:* Play as above but in pairs, trying to snatch partner's tail only.

6. *Beanbag Shuttle.* This is an ideal partner activity that provides challenge and agility. From a start line, space markers about 6 feet (2 m) apart in a column. Place 3 beanbags in a hoop positioned at end of markers, as shown. Set up 2 identical stations in this way. Have each partner stand behind a start line. On "Go!" signal, each partner runs in and out of the markers to pick up a beanbag, returns the same way, and places the beanbag just behind the start line. Challenge is over when all 3 beanbags are behind the start line. *Variation:* Return each beanbag, in turn, to the hoop.

COMMON FAULTS: DODGING

1. Eyes wander instead of staying focused in direction of travel.

2. Body stays too upright.

3. Not enough push off outside of foot.

4. More than one step is taken to create change direction.

5. Losing body control and falling over.

6. Changes of direction occur too slowly.

> **TEACHING TIPS: FIRST CORRECT THE COMPONENT THAT WILL HAVE THE GREATEST IMPACT.**
>
> ☛ Practical demonstration accompanied with simple and age-appropriate instruction is important when teaching children experiencing difficulties.
>
> ☛ Constant verbal and visual feedback are essential when trying to change poor movement components. This strategy is therefore applied to each and every one of these activities.
>
> ☛ Imagery can be useful in providing cues to correct movements.
>
> ☛ Motivation is essential for maintaining attention, interest, and participation.

ACTIVITIES TO CORRECT COMMON FAULTS

1. *Eyes wander instead of staying focused in direction of travel.*

➤ Have child focus forward on a target while dodging.

➤ Place a mark on your back on which child has to stay focused, and play Follow the Leader. Apart from just dodging, include other forms of locomotion.

➤ Verbally remind child to keep looking forward.

2. *Body stays too upright.*

➤ Ensure that child bends knees when changing direction.

➤ *Imagery:* Ask child to imagine that his or her legs are springs and that they spring into the direction change. (Most children will naturally bend their knees and lower their body.)

➤ May be necessary to have child widen the gap between the legs to achieve the desired result.

COMMON FAULTS: DODGING *(Continued)*

3. *Not enough push off the outside of foot.*

➤ Need to ensure that child is in fact pushing off the outside of this foot.

➤ Have the child face you with legs dodging-width apart. Ask child to alternately and continually push off from the outside of each foot. Check that the knees are kept bent.

➤ *Imagery:* Ask child to imagine that his or her legs are springs and that they spring into the direction change.

4. *More than one step is taken to create change direction.*

➤ Ask child to increase the force with which he or she pushes off with the legs.

➤ Have child face you with legs dodging-width apart. Ask child to alternately and continually push off from the inside of each foot. Check that the knees are kept bent.

➤ *Imagery:* Ask child to imagine that his or her legs are springs and that they spring into the direction change.

➤ Place a series of cones about 6 feet (2 m) apart. Parallel to these cones place a line dodging-width apart from the cones. Have child walk along the line; when child reaches level with a cone, push off hard to land next to it. Reverse direction to practice on both sides. Slowly increase speed.

5. *Losing body control and falling over.*

➤ Ensure that child has knees bent as he or she changes direction.

➤ Ensure that child is not leaning outside the support leg.

➤ Ensure that child does not move his or her head excessively.

6. *Changes of direction occur too slowly.*

➤ Ask child to increase the force with which he or she pushes off with the legs.

➤ Have child face you with legs dodging-width apart. Ask child to alternately and continually push off from the inside of each foot. Gradually increase the speed. Check that the knees are kept bent.

➤ *Imagery:* Ask child to imagine his or her legs are loaded springs and that they spring into the direction change the moment they hit the ground.

➤ Place a series of cones about 6 feet (2 m) apart. Parallel to these cones place a line dodging-width apart from the cones. Have child walk along the line; when child reaches level with a cone, push off hard to land next to it. Reverse direction to practice on both sides. Slowly increase speed.

DODGING

Outcome/ Appearance • Success • Consistency • Rhythm • Coordination	1. Head is up and eyes are focused straight ahead in direction movement.	2. Change of direction initiated by pushing off with outside of foot.	3. Push off is forceful.	4. Knee of supporting leg is bent as direction change occurs.	5. Body is lowered during direction change.	6. Balance is maintained.	7. Change of direction occurs quickly in one step.

Equipment Required:

➤ 5 cones

➤ Whistle

Procedure (Demonstrate the procedure as you explain):

➤ Place the cones in a straight line 3 meters (10 feet) apart.

➤ Walk child through the course emphasizing to stay on line between the markers, dodge each cone, and then come back on line.

➤ Stand to side and then the front to observe the action.

➤ Instruct child to run as fast as possible and dodge as quickly as possible.

➤ Go on whistle.

➤ Allow child to pause between each effort.

➤ Repeat until you have assessed all the criteria.

Outcome/Appearance:

SCORE 3   If the action appears well balanced and the change of direction is quick and smooth. (Achieved)

SCORE 2   If the action appears reasonably balanced but the change of direction is not quick. (Almost achieved)

SCORE 1   If the action lacks balance and quick direction changes. (Not yet achieved/developed)

Assessment of Individual Criteria (Example):

5. Body is lowered during direction change.

SCORE 3   On this movement if the body achieves this position the majority of the time. (Achieved)

SCORE 2   On this movement if the body achieves this position but it is inconsistent. (Almost achieved)

SCORE 1   On this movement if the body fails to achieve. (Not yet achieved/developed)

Assessment Tips:

➤ Encourage the child at all times, making the assessment as non-threatening as possible.

➤ Avoid distractions.

➤ Ensure the child experiences some success before ending the assessment.

➤ Ensure that wind is not a factor as dodging becomes difficult. Go inside if it is.

➤ Ensure the surface is firm and not wet.

DODGING

Name	Outcome/ Appearance • Success • Consistency • Rhythm • Coordination	1. Head is up and eyes focused straight ahead in direction movement.	2. Change of direction initiated by pushing off with out-side of foot.	3. Push off is forceful.	4. Knee of supporting leg is bent as direction change occurs.	5. Body is lowered during direction change.	6. Balance is main-tained.	7. Change of direction occurs quickly in one step.

HOPPING

PREPARING TO MOVE

1. Knee of the swinging leg is held in front of the body, but the foot is behind the body.
2. Arms are bent at right angles.
3. Body has a slight forward lean.
4. Head is up and eyes are looking forward.

MOVING

5. Hop starts on one foot and lands on the same foot.
6. Take-off and landing are on the forefoot.
7. Weight moves from the forefoot to the heel at landing.
8. Hopping leg bends to absorb the landing force, then extends to drive off the ground.
9. Swinging leg remains bent and moves back and forth during the hop, in opposition to the support leg, assisting in the forward movement.
10. Arms are bent and move upward and forward in opposition to the legs to assist in the hop.
11. Head remains up with the eyes looking forward.
12. Movement is continuous and rhythmical.

TEACHABLE POINTS

1. Head remains up and still with the eyes looking forward.
2. Knee of the non-supporting leg swings to produce force.
3. Foot is held behind the body.
4. Arms bent at 90° move actively in opposition to the driving leg.
5. Take-off and landing are on the forefoot.
6. Weight moves from the forefoot to the heel on landing.
7. Hopping leg bends to absorb the landing force.
8. Hopping leg extends strongly to drive off the ground.

92

HOPPING ACTIVITIES

You may need to offer support when necessary. Make sure the child practices with both legs, rather than favoring one leg. Hopping, like jumping, is a strenuous activity and should therefore be combined with other movements to avoid soreness and fatigue.

1. Have child practice single-leg balance activities.

2. Have child jump from two feet and land on one foot.

3. Ask child to hop in place, with support (such as holding a chair or parent). Repeat with hands out to side.

1.

4. Hop in front of a mirror to see self doing the action.

5. Have child hop in a swimming pool, if access to a pool is possible. This is an excellent strategy as it assists balance; also if the child is overweight, it decreases stress on the joints.

6. Together, hand in hand, hop with child.

6.

7. Hop certain distances using markers to determine the distance.

8. How many hops does it take to reach a certain spot?

9. Have child complete one hop and then balance in place with and then without the hands on the hips.

10. Ask child to hop low to the ground; hop higher and higher.

11. Have child hop in different directions: forwards, backwards, sideways.

12. Ask child to hop over low objects. Gradually increase the height.

12.

HOPPING CHALLENGES

1. *Hop-a-Pattern.* Have child change hopping foot frequently. Challenge child to show you how he or she can hop in a circle; a triangle; favorite number; favorite letter; the initials of his or her name; figure-8.

2. *Action Poem.* Together create an action poem. For example: Hop, hop, to the store; skip, skip all the way home; slide-slide to school; jump, jump up and down like a bouncing ball.

3. *Hopping Dance.* Together create a hopping dance. For example: Walk forward 4 steps; walk backwards 4 steps; do 2 hops in place with one foot, then other foot; skip around in a circle; then clap your hands and stamp your feet 3 times. Repeat!

RELATED GAMES

1. *Hopscotch.* Use masking tape or chalked lines to create a hopscotch pattern. Together establish rules for the game and play! Some examples are given here.

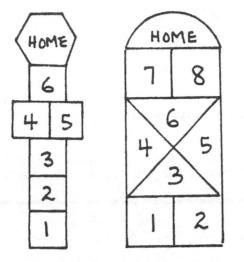

2. *Hopping Tag.* At least 3 players are needed to play this game. Confine the game to a small area. One player is the Tagger. Select different ways of having players move: walking, running, sliding, skipping. If tagged, that player must *hop* in place. Change the Tagger and start a new game.

COMMON FAULTS: HOPPING

1. Landing flat-footed or staying on the toes.
2. Taking off flat-footed.
3. Nonsupport leg too low or in front of the body.
4. Poor leg drive.
5. Inconsistent height and length of hop.
6. Poor balance.
7. No arm drive.
8. No opposing leg drive.
9. Head moves or the eyes are looking down.

TEACHING TIPS: FIRST CORRECT THE COMPONENT THAT WILL HAVE THE GREATEST IMPACT.

☛ Practical demonstration accompanied with simple and age-appropriate instruction is important when teaching children experiencing difficulties.

☛ Constant verbal and visual feedback are essential when trying to change poor movement components. This strategy is therefore applied to each and every one of these activities.

☛ Imagery can be useful in providing cues to correct movements.

☛ Motivation is essential for maintaining attention, interest, and participation.

ACTIVITIES TO CORRECT COMMON FAULTS

Note: Practice with both feet.

1. Landing too heavily.

➤ *Imagery:* Have child imagine that he or she is landing as lightly as possible.

➤ *Imagery:* As above but landing as quietly as possible.

2. Taking off flat-footed.

➤ Assist child as he or she alternately bends and straightens the knee as he or she goes down and then up on the toes. On the count of "3" hop. Repeat.

➤ Have child bend the knee and lean slightly forward with each hop and then extend forcefully.

3. Nonsupport leg too low or in front of the body.

➤ Gently hold child just underneath the knee.

➤ Verbally encourage child to keep this leg up.

COMMON FAULTS: HOPPING (Continued)

4. *Poor leg drive.*

➤ Include in child's program leg strength and abdominal exercises. (Refer to strengthening activities in Section 1.)

➤ Check child's weight and make a decision if weight control is necessary.

➤ Check to see if child has the correct amount of knee bend and adjust accordingly.

➤ Have child hop over low soft objects. Ensure there is no chance of tripping or injury through contact.

5. *Inconsistent height and length of hop.*

➤ Have child hop to spaced markers.

➤ Have child hop over soft moveable similar-height objects. There must be no chance of tripping or injury through contact.

6. *Poor balance.*

➤ Make sure child is not leaning too far forward during the hop.

➤ Make sure child does not have excessive upper body movements including the arms.

➤ Have child stop and balance between hops.

➤ Hold child's hand while hopping.

7. *No arm drive.*

➤ *Imagery:* Have child imagine that he or she is stirring two large bowls at the same time (elbows are bent). Initially do this while standing, then with single hops, and finally multiple hops.

8. *No opposing leg drive.*

(This is best achieved with verbal reminding and motivation.)

➤ Have child step forward with one leg and then drive with the knee of the opposite leg, landing on one foot.

➤ From an assisted single-leg balance position, have child repeat the above exercise.

9. *Head moves or the eyes are looking down.*

➤ Focus on a target while hopping.

➤ Have child gently hop with a beanbag on the head.

HOPPING

Outcome/ Appearance • Success • Consistency • Rhythm • Coordination	1. Head up and eyes looking forward.	2. Non-supporting knee swings to produce force.	3. Foot is held behind body.	4. Arms bent 90° and move actively in opposition to driving leg.	5. Take-off and landing are on forefoot.	6. Weight moves from forefoot to heel on landing.	7. Hopping leg bends to absorb landing force.	8. Hopping leg extends strongly to drive off ground.

Equipment Required:

➤ 2 marker cones

➤ Clear space

Procedure (Demonstrate the procedure as you explain):

➤ Place the cones 5 yards/meters apart.

➤ Ask child to hop from one cone to the other. Instruct child to then hop back on the other leg.

➤ Allow child to pause between each effort.

➤ Repeat until you have assessed all the criteria.

Outcome/Appearance:

SCORE 3   If the child lands balanced on the same foot when hopping and the action is rhythmical and forceful. **(Achieved)**

SCORE 2   If the child lands balanced on the same foot when hopping but the action may lack rhythm and/or force. **(Almost achieved)**

SCORE 1   If the child does not consistently land on the same foot, or overbalances. **(Not yet achieved/developed)**

Assessment of Individual Criteria (Example):

4. Arms bent 90° and move actively in opposition to driving leg.

SCORE 3   On this movement if the arms achieve this position and movement the majority of the time. **(Achieved)**

SCORE 2   On this movement if the arms achieve this position but it is inconsistent. **(Almost achieved)**

SCORE 1   On this movement if the arms fail to achieve this position or movement. **(Not yet achieved/developed)**

Assessment Tips:

➤ Make sure the surface is flat and firm and not slippery.

➤ Do not try to use directional terms such as left and right foot, when assessing young children as this wastes time. Use terms "same foot" and "other foot."

➤ Encourage the child at all times, making the assessment as non-threatening as possible.

➤ Avoid distractions.

➤ Ensure the child experiences some success before ending the assessment.

HOPPING

Name	Outcome/ Appearance • Success • Consistency • Rhythm • Coordination	1. Head up and eyes looking forward.	2. Non-supporting knee swings to produce force.	3. Foot is held behind body.	4. Arms bent 90° and actively move in opposition to driving leg.	5. Take-off and landing are on forefoot.	6. Weight moves from forefoot to heel on landing.	7. Hopping leg bends to absorb landing force.	8. Hopping leg extends strongly to drive off ground.

SKIPPING

MOVING

1. Skipping action is performed on the balls of the feet.

2. Knees remain slightly flexed.

3. Arms and legs move in opposition to each other.

4. Body leans slightly forward.

5. Hop looks low to the ground because the non-support leg remains close to the ground during the hop.

6. During the action, head remains up with eyes focused forward.

7. Movement appears rhythmical.

TEACHABLE POINTS

1. Head remains up with eyes looking forward during the action.

2. Step hop is evident.

3. Height and distance of steps and hops are consistent.

4. Body lean is slightly forward.

5. Landing is on the forefoot.

6. Arms move in opposition to the legs.

SKIPPING ACTIVITIES

Use music with a strong 4/4 beat to help establish the skipping rhythm. Choose a moderate tempo that the child can easily follow. (Practice hopping. If child has difficulties, refer to the section and activities on hopping.)

1. Place a series of markers on the ground and have child step to one marker and then hop to the next. Talk child through the movement slowly: "Step right, hop; step left, hop." Allow child to initially look at feet and then repeat the activity without looking at feet.

2. Repeat without markers.

3. Hold child's hand and skip in place saying: "Right hop, left hop, right hop, left hop," . . . .

4. Have child skip forward to music (slowly at first).

5. Ask child to skip forward, making slight changes of direction.

6. Ask child to show skipping in a happy way (swinging arms and lifting knees high).

7. Have child skip with changes of speed: slowly, quickly.

8. Have child skip forward around different obstacles.

9. Have child hold hands with you or a partner and skip forward together.

10. Combine skipping with other movements: skipping—jumping—skipping—sliding.

11. Try the above activities skipping backwards.

SKIPPING CHALLENGES

1. *Skip, Skip.* Skip, skip to the goal post; hop, hop to the tree; jump, jump to the wall; run, run all around the basketball court.

2. *Skipping Patterns.* Skip in a circle; in a square; in a figure-8; and so on.

3. *Skipping Dance.* Make up a dance with skipping as the main action. Have child skip alone; skip while holding hands in a circle; skip forwards and backwards.

SKIPPING GAMES

1. *Shark Attack!* Scatter several hoops throughout a defined play area. Choose 3 players to be the sharks, who each hold a beanbag. Players ("fish") move ("swim") around the play area by skipping. Sharks try to catch (tag) free players with their beanbags. Players can jump into any hoop to be safe. Only one player per hoop. After 3-second count "one shark, two sharks, three sharks," player must leave hoop. Fish that are caught must jog in place. After a certain time, count all the fish that the sharks caught. Choose new sharks and play again!

SKIPPING GAMES *(Continued)*

2. *Poison Circle.* Mark out a large circle as the play area. All players stand inside the circle to start the game. On the signal "Scrambled Eggs—Skip!" players skip around and pretend that everyone is poison. If a player touches you, then you are "poisoned" and must continue skipping with one hand behind your back; if touched again, the other hand must be put behind your back.

COMMON FAULTS: SKIPPING

1. Landing too flat-footed and heavy.

2. Inconsistent heights and distances of hop and steps.

3. Cannot hop; therefore, cannot skip.

4. Swing leg too high off the ground.

5. Poor balance.

6. Too much forward lean of the body.

7. Arms not synchronized in opposition with the legs.

8. Moving the head during the action.

TEACHING TIPS: FIRST CORRECT THE COMPONENT THAT WILL HAVE THE GREATEST IMPACT.

☛ Practical demonstration accompanied with simple and age-appropriate instruction is important when teaching children experiencing difficulties.

☛ Constant verbal and visual feedback are essential when trying to change poor movement components. This strategy is therefore applied to each and every one of these activities.

☛ Imagery can be useful in providing cues to correct movements.

☛ Motivation is essential for maintaining attention, interest, and participation.

COMMON FAULTS: SKIPPING (*Continued*)

ACTIVITIES TO CORRECT COMMON FAULTS

1. Landing too flat-footed and heavy.

➤ If child can perform the skipping action, ask him or her to skip as quietly and softly as possible. Show child how this is best achieved by stepping on the forefoot.

➤ Have child raise up onto the forefoot and take one step, one hop, and then place the foot down. Repeat on the cue: "Up—Step—Hop—Down."

➤ Have child move slowly through the action as described above saying these cue words. Remind child: "Heels up." Have child gradually increase speed.

➤ Use constant verbal reminding of "Heels up!"

2. Inconsistent heights and distances of hop and steps.

➤ Ask child to skip as *high* as possible and then as *low* as possible. This will make the child concentrate on consistency.

➤ Mark out a square so that each side is covered in about 4–6 skips. Tell child to make sure he or she has the same number of skips along each side. Review numbers and discuss after each circuit.

➤ *Imagery:* Ask child to imagine that she or he is skipping in shallow water and the feet are not allowed to come above the surface.

3. Cannot hop; therefore, cannot skip. (This is not always the case.)

➤ If child cannot balance, have child practice single-leg balancing activities.

➤ Ask child to hop and balance for 2 seconds. Repeat using both legs.

➤ Have child take one step and then hop and try to balance on one leg. Then do the same with the other leg. Gradually decrease the time of balance.

4. Swing leg too high off the ground.

➤ *Imagery:* Ask child to imagine that he or she is skipping in shallow water and the feet are not allowed to come above the surface. You can use similar ideas.

5. Poor balance.

➤ Ensure that child does not lean his or her upper body too far forward in the skip.

➤ Start child skipping on the spot, gradually increasing the distance between the step-hop.

➤ Ensure that the head is not moving excessively and remains up in the skip. A soft beanbag placed on the head can assist this.

COMMON FAULTS: SKIPPING *(Continued)*

➤ Ensure child is landing with the knee slightly bent.

➤ Place a series of markers on the ground and have child step to one marker and then hop to the next. Balance on each hop. Talk child through the movement slowly: "Step right, hop, and balance." Slowly increase the speed and decrease the balance period.

6. *Too much forward lean of the body.*

➤ *Imagery:* Ask child to imagine that he or she has a string attached to the back and is being pulled slightly backwards.

➤ Ensure that the head is not moving excessively and remains up in the skip. A soft beanbag placed on the head can assist this.

➤ *Imagery:* Have child imagine that his or her chest *just* leads or is in front of the stomach.

7. *Arms not synchronized in opposition with the legs.*

➤ Take child's hands and guide him or her through the correct action as he or she slowly skips.

➤ Have child march and call the arm action. Change from march to skip action.

➤ As child moves a leg forward, ask child to place his or her hand on the hip of the same side. This is done alternately as child skips.

8. *Moving the head during the action.*

➤ Focus on a target while skipping.

➤ Have child skip with a beanbag on the head.

➤ Place a mark on your back on which the child has to stay focused, and play Follow the Leader. Apart from just skipping, include or even start with other forms of locomotion.

➤ Verbally remind child to keep looking forward.

SKIPPING

Outcome/ Appearance • Success • Consistency • Rhythm • Coordination	1. Head up, still, and eyes looking forward.	2. Step hop is evident.	3. Height and distance of steps and hops are consistent.	4. Body lean is slightly forward.	5. Lands on forefoot.	6. Arms move in opposition to legs.

Equipment Required:

➤ 2 markers
➤ Large open space

Procedure: (Demonstrate the process as you explain):

➤ Place the markers about 5 yards/meters apart.
➤ Ask child to skip on your command from one marker to the other.
➤ Ask child to skip back to the original marker.
➤ Allow child to pause between efforts.
➤ Repeat until you have assessed all the criteria.

Outcome/Appearance:

SCORE 3   If the child can skip and the action appears rhythmical. (Achieved)

SCORE 2   If the child can skip, although the action may lack rhythm. (Almost achieved)

SCORE 1   If the child is unable to skip. (Not yet achieved/developed)

Assessment of Individual Criteria (Example):

2. Step hop is evident.

SCORE 3   On this movement if this combination is evident the majority of the time. (Achieved)

SCORE 2   On this movement if this combination is evident, but it is inconsistent. (Almost achieved)

SCORE 1   On this movement if the child fails to achieve this combination. (Not yet achieved/developed)

Assessment Tips:

➤ Ensure that the surface is level and firm.
➤ Encourage the child at all times, making the assessment as non-threatening as possible.
➤ Avoid distractions.
➤ Ensure the child experiences some success before ending the assessment.

SKIPPING

SCORE 3: Achieved
SCORE 2: Almost achieved
SCORE 1: Not yet achieved/developed

Name	Outcome/ Appearance • Success • Consistency • Rhythm • Coordination	1. Head up, still, and eyes looking forward.	2. Step hop is evident.	3. Height and distance of steps and hops are consistent.	4. Body lean is slightly forward.	5. Lands on forefoot.	6. Arms move in opposition to legs.

LEAPING

MOVING

1. Leaping action is done on the balls of the feet and is a spring from one foot, landing on the other or both.

2. Knees and ankles bend at landing to absorb the force of the landing.

3. Arms assist in the propulsion by extending forward and upward vigorously as the legs extend forcefully.

4. Body leans slightly forward during flight.

5. Lead foot lands softly on the ball of the foot (forefoot) without losing balance.

6. During the action, head remains up with eyes focused forward.

7. Movement looks rhythmical and uninterrupted.

TEACHABLE POINTS

1. Head remains up with eyes looking forward during the action.

2. Arms assist and are synchronized in opposition to the legs.

3. Take off is on one foot; landing is on the opposite foot.

4. Landing is on the forefoot.

5. Knees bend slightly to absorb force on landing.

6. Balance is maintained on landing.

LEAPING ACTIVITIES

1. Have child run forward and leap off one foot into the air, landing softly on two feet. Repeat, leaping off the other foot. Try to convey the feeling of "flying" through the air.

1. "FLYING"

2. Have child step and leap off that foot to grab or touch something high with both hands and land softly on opposite foot. Emphasize using arms to help reach upward and bending at knees to absorb force. Repeat leaping off the other foot.

3. Repeat activity 2 but explore leaping upwards with leg and arm on the same side; on opposite sides. Which is better?

3.　　　　4.

4. Have child leap over a line or stretched rope, landing on opposite foot. Explore leaping over the line with one foot, then the other.

5. Set up 4–6 long ropes, spaced about 1 m apart. Have child leap over the ropes, changing leading foot. Observe that "opposite arm to opposite leg" occurs.

7.

6. Remove the ropes and have child leap in a straight line, over a set distance. Count the number of leaps taken.

7. Using two stretched ropes as shown, have child leap over the 2 ropes. Gradually increase the distance between the ropes. Land on opposite foot each time.

8.

8. Set up low obstacles or a rope or pole stretched between 2 chairs. Have child leap over the obstacles. Encourage leaping with either foot. Emphasize good landings. Use chalk to mark out a take-off board or draw a line in the sand. Have child run toward the board, take-off on one foot, landing on opposite foot. Landing should be on grass, sand, or, if possible, a mat.

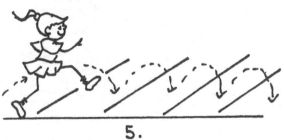

5.

LEAPING CHALLENGES

1. *Alligator Leap.* Set 2 long ropes at an angle to each other as shown, about 1 m at the narrow end and 3 m at the wide end. Have child attempt to leap across the "river" which is full of alligators. With each successful leap, child can attempt to leap across the wider parts.

2. *Circle Leap.* Using a long rope with a beanbag tied at one end, swing the rope in a circle, gently and low to the ground. Have child leap over the rope. Gradually swing the rope higher off the ground and quicker.

3. *Bridge Leap.* Suspend a rope between two chairs. Have child leap over the rope. Start quite low, then gradually suspend the rope higher off the ground.

4. *Leap and Tap.* Suspend a ball in a nylon stocking from a tree or other suitable fixture. Have child leap up to tap the ball. Gradually raise the height of the ball.

5. *Long Jump Leap.* Use chalk to mark out a take-off board or draw a line in the sand. Have child run towards the board, take-off on one foot, landing on two feet. Landing should be on grass, sand, or, if possible, a mat. Mark distance jumped each time.

ALLIGATOR LEAP

CIRCLE LEAP

LEAP & TAP

LONG JUMP LEAP

COMMON FAULTS: LEAPING

1. Landing is too flat-footed and heavy.

2. Too much forward lean of the body.

3. Arms not synchronized in opposition with the legs when continuously leaping.

4. Poor balance.

5. Moving the head during the action.

TEACHING TIPS: FIRST CORRECT THE COMPONENT THAT WILL HAVE THE GREATEST IMPACT.

☛ Practical demonstration accompanied with simple and age-appropriate instruction is important when teaching children experiencing difficulties.

☛ Constant verbal and visual feedback are essential when trying to change poor movement components. This strategy is therefore applied to each and every one of these activities.

☛ Imagery can be useful in providing cues to correct movements.

☛ Motivation is essential for maintaining attention, interest, and participation.

ACTIVITIES TO CORRECT COMMON FAULTS

1. Landing is too flat-footed and heavy.

➤ While this skill is being developed, ensure that child lands on a soft surface and the knees bend on landing.

➤ Start with small jumps and ask child to land as softly and quietly as he or she can. At this stage you can offer suggestions as to how this can be achieved.

➤ Ask child to lean well forward as he or she lands. This will assist in the correct landing.

2. Too much forward lean of the body.

➤ Ensure that the head is not moving excessively and remains up in the leap. A soft beanbag placed on the head can assist this.

➤ *Imagery:* Have child imagine that his or her chest leads or is in front of the stomach.

3. Arms not synchronized in opposition with the legs when continuously leaping.

➤ Tell child to place the nondriving arm on the chest as he or she jumps. Repeat on both sides of the body.

COMMON FAULTS: LEAPING *(Continued)*

➤ Have child perform a single leap and call the arm action. Slowly increase the number of consecutive leaps with the call of the arm action. "Reach".

4. *Poor balance.*

➤ Ensure that child does not lean the upper body too far forward in the leap.

➤ Start child leaping short distances and landing with the opposing arm in front and the trailing arm slightly bent and out to the side for balance.

➤ Ensure that the head is not moving excessively and remains up in the leap. A soft beanbag placed on the head can assist this.

➤ Ensure child is landing with the knees slightly bent.

5. *Moving the head during the action.*

➤ Focus on a target while leaping.

➤ Have child leap with a beanbag on his or her head. Even if the beanbag drops off, the required result will be achieved if child is trying to keep it from dropping.

➤ Place a mark on your back on which child has to stay focused, and play Follow the Leader. Apart from just leaping, include other forms of locomotion.

➤ Verbally remind child to keep looking forward.

LEAPING

Outcome/ Appearance • Success • Consistency • Rhythm • Coordination	1. Head up and eyes looking forward.	2. Arms assist and are synchronized in opposition to legs.	3. Takes off on one foot and lands on opposite foot.	4. Lands on forefoot.	5. Knee(s) bend slightly to absorb force on landing.	6. Maintains balance on landing.

Equipment Required:

➤ 2 cones

➤ Masking tape

➤ Cleared area

Procedure (Demonstrate the process as you explain):

➤ Place one cone as a starting point; allow for a short run and mark a takeoff box.

➤ Ask child to run and leap as far as possible.

➤ Mark this spot and encourage child to improve the previous effort.

➤ Allow child to pause between efforts.

➤ Repeat until you have assessed all the criteria.

Outcome/Appearance:

SCORE 3   If the child maintains a smooth continuous forward movement and lands correctly. **(Achieved)**

SCORE 2   If the child lacks some continuity of forward movement but lands on the correct foot. Overbalance may also occur. **(Almost achieved)**

SCORE 1   If the child cannot take off correctly and land on the correct foot. Overbalance may also occur. **(Not yet achieved/developed)**

Assessment of Individual Criteria (Example):

2. Arms assist and are synchronized in opposition to legs.

SCORE 3   On this movement if the arms achieve this action consistently. **(Achieved)**

SCORE 2   On this movement if the arms achieve this action but it is inconsistent. **(Almost achieved)**

SCORE 1   On this movement if the arms fail to achieve this action. **(Not yet achieved/developed)**

Assessment Tips:

➤ Ensure the takeoff area is firm, flat, and not slippery.

➤ Ensure the landing area is suitably soft.

➤ Do not attempt assessment on a day that is too windy as balance may be affected.

➤ Encourage the child at all times, making the assessment as non-threatening as possible.

➤ Avoid distractions.

➤ Ensure the child experiences some success before ending the assessment.

LEAPING

Name	Outcome/ Appearance • Success • Consistency • Rhythm • Coordination	1. Head up and eyes looking forward.	2. Arms assist and are synchronized in opposition to legs.	3. Takes off on one foot and lands on opposite foot.	4. Lands on forefoot.	5. Knee(s) bend slightly to absorb force on landing.	6. Maintains balance on landing.

SLIDE-STEPPING

PREPARING TO MOVE

1. Body is turned and will remain sideways to the intended direction of travel with the feet together.

2. Head should be kept up with the eyes focused in the direction of travel.

MOVING

3. Leading leg side-steps, followed by a sliding action of the trailing leg back to the leading leg.

4. The move is on the forefoot.

5. Support alternates between the lead to the trailing leg.

6. Feet are kept close to the ground with a short time when both feet are off the ground.

7. Knees are kept slightly bent.

8. Side-step should be approximately shoulder-width apart.

9. Movement should be smooth and rhythmical.

10. Arms remain relaxed but may assist the movement.

11. Head is up with the eyes focused in the direction of travel.

TEACHABLE POINTS

1. Head is held up, still, and eyes look in the direction of travel.

2. A step and then a slide are evident.

3. Width of slide step is not too wide or too narrow.

4. Slide step is on the forefoot.

5. Knees are slightly bent throughout the action.

6. Body is side-on.

7. Arms remain passive.

8. Child can slide both ways.

SLIDE-STEPPING ACTIVITIES

Initially do activities facing child and stepping out the action; then stand next to each other. Start slowly and gradually get faster. At first allow child to look at his or her feet until the action becomes automatic.

1. Guide child slowly through the sequence: "Step to the side, feet together."

2. Initially allow the step to be exaggerated. Then reduce the size of the step.

3. Reverse direction, going through the same steps. Now the other foot leads the action.

4. Repeat #1–3 using a small leap.

5. Speed up the action using the command "side, together." Demonstrate.

6. Have child slide-step to music.

7. Have child slide-step to the right; slide-step to the left. On signal, "Jump-stop!"

8. Set up different obstacles for child to slide-step around.

9. Have child slide-step in a big circle; slide in zig-zag pattern; slide-step forward, backward.

10. Side by side with child, slide-step together as you hold hands.

11. Face each other, and mirror slide-stepping movements.

12. Combine slide-step with skips, hops, walks, and other movements.

SIDE   TOGETHER   SIDE
1-2

SLIDE   7.   JUMP STOP

10.

11.

8.

RELATED GAMES

1. ***Shadows.*** Use music to start and stop. Start with the slide-stepping movement, then use other locomotor movements. Have children find a partner and free space. With a partner, face each other, spaced about one giant step apart. One partner will be the Leader first; the other partner is the "Shadow." When the music is played, the Leader slide-steps around in general space, while the Shadow follows. When the music stops, both jump-stop. Change the Leader and Shadow frequently.

2. ***Chasey.*** Play simple tag using the slide-step movement. Have a "safe" position by freezing for a 3-second count in a static balance such as a "Stork Stand."*Variations:* Use other locomotor movements. Or play as above, but pair up players who must hold hands as they slide-step around.

3. ***Create a Dance.*** Use the slide-step and other locomotor movements to make a dance. For example, play music with a steady 4/4 beat and walk forward for 4 counts; walk backward for 4 counts; slide-step 4 counts to right, then 4 counts to the left; skip in a circle for 4 counts; and jump in place for 2 counts, 2 claps. Start again.

COMMON FAULTS: SLIDE-STEPPING

1. Moving flat-footed.

2. Crossing feet because child leads with the wrong foot.

3. Not shifting the weight from the lead to following foot, causing a stuttering movement.

4. Side-stepping too wide or too narrow.

5. Leaping too high.

6. Legs too straight.

7. Arms making unwanted movements.

8. Turning the trunk and/or feet to face the direction of travel.

TEACHING TIPS: FIRST CORRECT THE COMPONENT THAT WILL HAVE THE GREATEST IMPACT.

- Practical demonstration accompanied with simple and age-appropriate instruction is important when teaching children experiencing difficulties.
- Constant verbal and visual feedback are essential when trying to change poor movement components. This strategy is therefore applied to each and every one of these activities.
- Imagery can be useful in providing cues to correct movements.
- Motivation is essential for maintaining attention, interest, and participation.

ACTIVITIES TO CORRECT COMMON FAULTS

1. Moving flat-footed.

➤ If child can perform the sliding action, ask him or her to slide as quietly and softly as possible. Show child that this is best achieved on the forefoot.

➤ Have child raise up onto the forefoot and take one side-step, then place the foot down. Repeat on the cue words: "Up–Slide–Down."

➤ Have child move slowly through the action as described above but without the cue. Heels up. Gradually increase speed.

➤ Use constant verbal reminding to cue the "heels up."

2. Crossing feet because child leads with the wrong foot.

➤ It may be necessary to ask child to relax his or her feet and for you to physically take child through the correct action.

➤ Face child and have him or her mirror your actions. Gradually increase speed.

➤ Verbally remind child to use cue words: "Slide apart–Slide together."

COMMON FAULTS: SLIDE-STEPPING *(Continued)*

3. *Not shifting the weight from the lead to following foot, causing a stuttering movement.*

   ➤ Ask child to lift his or her lead leg and momentarily hold a balanced position, and then place the lead foot on the ground. Use the verbal cue: "Lift–Hold–Step, and Slide." Gradually increase speed.

   ➤ Encourage child to feel that he or she is leaning slightly away from the direction of the slide, which will place more weight on the trailing leg.

4. *Side-stepping too wide or too narrow.*

   ➤ *Imagery:* Ask child to imagine or feel that he or she is stepping as wide apart as the shoulders.

   ➤ Place floor markers on the ground and ask child to slide from marker to marker. Gradually increase speed.

   ➤ Face child and have him or her mirror your sliding movements.

   ➤ Give verbal cues to increase the size of the step.

5. *Leaping too high.*

   ➤ *Imagery:* Ask child to pretend that he or she is on a carpet of air just off the ground.

   ➤ *Imagery:* Imagine that there is a large sheet of glass a few inches (cm) off the ground. Child must try to keep his or her feet under this sheet.

   ➤ Verbally remind child using the cue words: "Low and long."

6. *Legs too straight.*

   ➤ *Imagery:* Ask child to slide as softly and quietly as possible. Experiment with straight legs and bent knees using some guided discovery to achieve the desired outcome.

   ➤ Have child place his or her hands on knees and slowly slide-step. If child tries to do this with straight legs, it will feel uncomfortable. Discuss with child how it is easier when the knees are slightly bent.

   ➤ Use verbal reminding cue: "Springy knees."

7. *Arms making unwanted movements.*

   ➤ Hold hands with child while sliding.

   ➤ Have child deliberately hold his or her hands to the side or front while sliding and verbally remind child if the arms move.

   ➤ *Imagery:* Have child pretend that he or she is holding hands with a person on either side or in front.

8. *Turning the trunk and/or feet to face the direction of travel.*

   ➤ Hold hands with child while sliding.

   ➤ Have child mirror you sliding.

   ➤ *Imagery:* Have child move sideways like a crab.

   ➤ Use verbal reminding cue: "Shoulders first."

SLIDE-STEPPING

Outcome/ Appearance • Success • Consistency • Rhythm • Coordination	1. Head up, still, and eyes looking in direction of travel.	2. A step and then slide are evident.	3. Width of slide-step is not too wide or too narrow.	4. Slide-step is on forefoot.	5. Knees are slightly bent throughout action.	6. Body is side-on.	7. Arms remain passive.	8. Can slide both ways.

Equipment required:

➤ 2 marker cones
➤ Large cleared area

Procedure (Demonstrate the procedure as you explain):

➤ Place the markers about 5 yards/meters apart.
➤ Ask child to face you and slide-step on your command from one marker to the other.
➤ Still facing you, ask child to slide-step back to the original marker.
➤ Allow child to pause between efforts.
➤ Repeat until you have assessed all the criteria.

Outcome/Appearance:

SCORE 3   If the child can slide-step in both directions and the action appears rhythmical. **(Achieved)**

SCORE 2   If the child can slide-step in at least one direction. The action may lack rhythm. **(Almost achieved)**

SCORE 1   If the child is unable to slide-step. **(Not yet achieved/developed)**

Assessment of Individual Criteria (Example):

6. Body is sideways.

SCORE 3   On this movement if the body achieves this position the majority of the time. **(Achieved)**

SCORE 2   On this movement if the body achieves this position but it is inconsistent. **(Almost achieved)**

SCORE 1   On this movement if the body fails to achieve this position. **(Not yet achieved/developed)**

Assessment Tips:

➤ Ensure the surface is firm and not slippery.
➤ Do not try to use directional terms such as "left" and "right" when assessing young children as this wastes time. Use terms "same" and "other direction."
➤ Encourage the child at all times, making the assessment as non-threatening as possible.
➤ Avoid distractions.
➤ Ensure the child experiences some success before ending the assessment.

SLIDE-STEPPING

Name	Outcome/ Appearance • Success • Consistency • Rhythm • Coordination	1. Head up, still, and eyes looking in direction of travel.	2. A step and then slide are evident.	3. Width of slide-step is not too wide or too nar-row.	4. Slide-step is on forefoot.	5. Knees are slightly bent throughout action.	6. Body is side-on.	7. Arms remain passive.	8. Can slide both ways.

SECTION 4

OBJECT-CONTROL SKILLS

CATCHING: RECEIVING A ROLLED BALL (Prerequisite Stage—Large Ball)

PREPARING TO MOVE

1. In a balanced position, stand facing the thrower, feet shoulder-width apart.
2. Knees comfortably flexed.
3. Eyes focused on the ball thrower.

MOVING

4. Feet must move to get the body in a position behind the ball.
5. Knees bend; bottom should be close to the ground.
6. Arms and hands must be extended downwards to receive the oncoming ball.
7. Distance between the hands is determined by the size of ball.
8. Fingers should be spread, slightly curved and facing downwards to receive the ball.
9. Ball should be scooped into the body.
10. Ball should be tracked with the eyes at all times.

TEACHABLE POINTS

1. Eyes are focused on the ball source and track the ball along the ground.
2. Child moves to get the body behind the ball.
3. Fingers are spread and face downwards ready to receive the oncoming ball.
4. Preferred leg is in front and knees bend to get down to the ball.
5. Child takes the ball cleanly in the hands.

125

RECEIVING A ROLLED BALL ACTIVITIES

Balls such as netball-size balls, or soft balls such as "gator" balls, are ideal for these activities.

1. To develop visual tracking, have child lie on his or her back tracking a ball in a stocking that you dangle above him or her. Child tries to hit at the stocking with one hand and then the other.

2. Demonstrate the receiving position. Have child copy you.

3. Have child practice moving down into the receiving position from standing still to bending at the knees. Repeat, going down on one knee. Let child decide which is more comfortable.

4. Physically take child's hands and place them in the correct position. While child holds this position, bring the ball into the hands and observe the reaction of the fingers. Ensure that the fingers are spread and relaxed with the fingers facing downwards. Repeat several times until mastered.

5. Sit on the ground, facing child, both with legs straddled apart. Roll the ball towards child asking him or her to keep eyes fixed on the ball. Check for hands in the correct position to receive the ball.

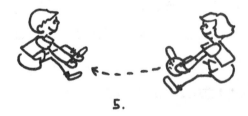

6. Now repeat #5 in kneeling position. Repeat with one knee up, the other down.

RECEIVING A ROLLED BALL ACTIVITIES

(Continued)

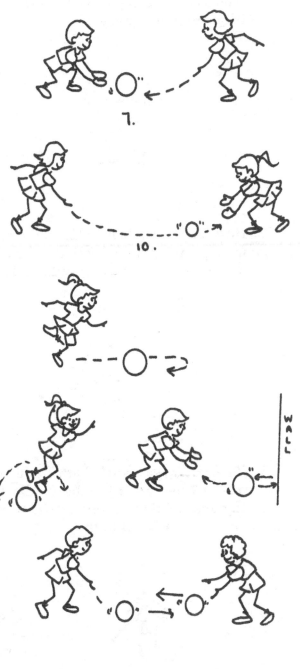

7. Repeat #5 in a standing position. At this stage, emphasize the importance of bending from the knees to reach down to the ball.

8. Repeat #7, gradually increasing the distance between you and child.

9. Increase the difficulty by varying the speed and direction of the roll.

10. When child has mastered receiving a large ball, try using a smaller ball.

11. Try these rolling stunts:

    ➤ Roll the ball ahead. How many times can you jump back and forth over the ball?

    ➤ Show me how you run after the ball, get in front of it, and field it in your hands.

    ➤ Roll ball at a wall. Field it with your hands.

    ➤ Roll ball into a box. Start near box, then gradually get further away from the box.

    ➤ With a partner, space yourselves 4 giant steps apart. Each roll a ball at the same time to the other partner. Now watch the fun!

    ➤ Sit down facing your partner, and roll a ball as quickly as you can, back and forth to each other.

    ➤ Keep the ball rolling! Don't let it touch any of the other rolling balls.

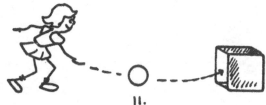

RELATED GAMES

1. ***Rolling Soccer.*** Using some kind of marker (such as bricks or cans), make goals 3 meters apart and just in front of a wall. Have partners take turns being the roller who stands 4 meters away and tries to roll the ball between the goals. Goalie uses hands to protect the goals.

2. ***Bowling Roll.*** Mark a line and place 3 plastic jugs about 5 meters away. Arrange the jugs in a pyramid fashion. Have child roll the ball towards the jugs trying to knock them over. Increase rolling distance as rolling skill is mastered.

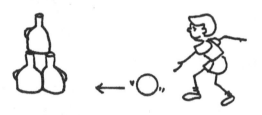

3. ***Partner Target Roll.*** Partners stand facing about 6 meters apart with 2 markers spaced 1 meter apart in the middle. Partners roll ball back and forth between the markers, fielding it properly with hands. *Variation:* Sit down, facing each other, and roll a ball back and forth.

RELATED GAMES *(Continued)*

4. *Hot Potato.* Ideally played with 5 players in a group who knee-sit in a circle. Choose one of the players to start the game and hold a small ball. The ball is a "hot potato." As the ball is rolled to a player, he or she gently bats it away before the ball can touch that player. If the Hot Potato does touch a player, then that player must run around the circle and return to his or her place to continue to play the game. *Remember:* Do not let the ball bounce along the floor. *Send ball to a player who is not sitting on either side of you, or to a player who just rolled the ball to you.*

5. *Ball Race.* Roll a ball along the ground or floor in a large open space. Challenge child to race the ball, trying to get ahead of it!

6. *Jump the Ball.* Play with 3 players. Two players stand facing each other, spaced 5 giant steps apart. The other player stands in the middle. Two outside players roll the ball back and forth to each other, while the middle player tries to jump or leap over the ball. After 5 jumps, change roles until everyone has had a turn in the middle.

COMMON FAULTS:
RECEIVING A ROLLED BALL

1. In an attempt to get down to the ball, child bends just from the waist without bending the knees.

2. Poor positioning of the body and hands in relation to the oncoming ball (not behind the ball).

3. Too much tension in the hands and fingers.

4. Fingers are not facing down to the ground.

5. Hands close too slowly or too quickly.

6. Not following the ball with the eyes.

> **TEACHING TIPS: FIRST CORRECT THE COMPONENT THAT WILL HAVE THE GREATEST IMPACT.**
>
> ☛ Practical demonstration accompanied with simple and age-appropriate instruction is important when teaching children experiencing difficulties.
>
> ☛ Constant verbal and visual feedback are essential when trying to change poor movement components. This strategy is therefore applied to each and every one of these activities.
>
> ☛ Imagery can be useful in providing cues to correct movements.
>
> ☛ Motivation is essential for maintaining attention, interest, and participation.

ACTIVITIES TO CORRECT COMMON FAULTS

1. *In an attempt to get down to the ball, child bends just from the waist without bending the knees.*

   ➤ Verbally remind child to bend his or her knees while receiving the ball.

   ➤ Use verbal cues such as: "Bend knees and lower."

   ➤ Flexibility exercises for the hamstrings and lower back may be needed in the program if bending is a problem. (Refer to Section 1.) Tell child to place the leg opposite the preferred throwing hand in front of the other leg. This makes it easier to lower to the ball.

2. *Poor positioning of the body and hands in relation to the oncoming ball (not behind the ball).*

   ➤ Have child move sideways to a rolled ball and try to stop it with his or her legs. Slowly increase the speed of the roll.

COMMON FAULTS:
RECEIVING A ROLLED BALL *(Continued)*

➤ Place 4 markers 6 feet (2 m) in front of child and space each marker 3 feet (1 m) apart. Instruct child to stand in line with the middle of the inner 2 markers. Tell child that when the ball comes through the middle markers, he or she does not have to move. When it is rolled through either of the side markers, then child must move to that side as soon as the ball passes the markers.

➤ A similar result can be achieved by using masking tape to mark lanes on the ground.

➤ Sit on the ground, facing child, both with legs straddled apart. Roll the ball towards child, asking him or her to keep eyes fixed on the ball. Check for hands in the correct position to receive the ball.

➤ Now repeat previous activity in kneeling position. Repeat with one knee up, the other down.

➤ Repeat activity in a standing position. At this stage, emphasize the importance of bending from the knees to reach down to the ball.

3. *Too much tension in the hands and fingers.*

➤ Sometimes tension is inherent. Child needs to practice relaxation exercises and can be trained to feel tension so he or she can learn to relax. Stress balls are useful for this.

➤ Verbally remind child to relax and shake the hands and fingers to release the tension before receiving the ball.

➤ *Imagery:* Tell child to imagine that he or she is receiving an egg and must not break it.

4. *Fingers are not facing down to the ground.*

➤ Provide constant verbal reminding to place the fingers downwards.

➤ Physically take child's hands and place them in the correct position. While child holds this position, bring the ball into the hands and observe the reaction of the fingers. Ensure that the fingers are spread and relaxed with the fingers facing downwards.

➤ Repeat several times until mastered. Repeat in a kneeling position; then in standing position.

5. *Hands close too slowly or too quickly.*

➤ Play the game of Grab. Stand in front of child with a ball. If child is too slow with the hand action, hold the ball out in front and balanced on the palm, with child's hands to the side of the ball. Tell child that you are going to take your hand away and drop the ball and he or she has to try and grab it before it drops.

COMMON FAULTS:
RECEIVING A ROLLED BALL *(Continued)*

➤ Hold the ball in front of child and have him or her try to move the hands quickly to grab it from you as you move it around.

➤ If child is too quick, use slow-moving objects such as balloons and scarves and verbally remind child not to "snatch at the ball."

➤ While rolling the ball to child, verbally remind him or her by using cue words such as "quick hands" or "no snatching."

6. *Not following the ball with the eyes.*

➤ Have child lie on his or her back and complete eye-tracking exercises using a ball on a string. It is useful to have child strike the ball intermittently to improve eye-hand coordination.

➤ Working with slow floating objects such as scarves and balloons can improve child's eye tracking.

➤ Give constant verbal reminding for child to watch the ball.

RECEIVING A ROLLED BALL

Outcome/ Appearance • Success • Consistency • Rhythm • Coordination	1. Eyes focused on ball source and track ball along ground.	2. Moves to get body behind ball.	3. Fingers spread and face down-wards ready to receive oncom-ing ball.	4. Preferred leg in front and knees bend to get down to ball.	5. Takes ball cleanly in hands.

Equipment Required:

➤ Volleyballs or balls of similar size

➤ Masking tape

Procedure (Demonstrate the procedure as you explain):

➤ Clear a flat level area and place a meter strip of masking tape on the ground and anoth-er piece 5 meters (15 ft) away.

➤ Have child stand behind the masking tape and roll the ball firmly towards him or her.

➤ Repeat until you have assessed all the criteria.

➤ The ball can then be rolled to the side of child to assess if child moves his or her feet to get behind the ball and receive it.

➤ Thank the child for his or her effort.

Outcome/Appearance:

SCORE 3   If child displays anticipation and successfully controls the ball consistently. **(Achieved)**

SCORE 2   If child receives the ball but does not always control the ball correctly and cleanly. **(Almost achieved)**

SCORE 1   If child displays inconsistent and incorrect ball control. **(Not yet achieved/developed)**

Assessment of Individual Criteria (Example):

3. Fingers spread and face downwards ready to receive oncoming ball.

SCORE 3   On this movement if the fingers achieve this position the majority of the time. **(Achieved)**

SCORE 2   On this movement if the fingers achieve this position but it is inconsistent. **(Almost achieved)**

SCORE 1   On this movement if the fingers fail to achieve this position. **(Not yet achieved/developed)**

Assessment Tips:

➤ You may wish to have a third person roll the ball so that assessment may be easier.

➤ Reduce distractions.

➤ Provide motivation and encouragement.

➤ Ensure that the surface is level.

➤ Tell the child when you are about to roll the ball.

➤ Ensure that the child experiences some success before the assessment ends.

RECEIVING A ROLLED BALL

SCORE 3: Achieved
SCORE 2: Almost achieved
SCORE 1: Not yet achieved/developed

Name	Outcome/ Appearance • Success • Consistency • Rhythm • Coordination	1. Eyes focused on ball source and track ball along ground.	2. Moves to get body behind ball.	3. Fingers spread and face downwards ready to receive oncoming ball.	4. Preferred leg in front and knees bend to get down to ball.	5. Takes ball cleanly in hands.

BOUNCING AND CATCHING WITH TWO HANDS
(Large Ball)

PREPARING TO MOVE

1. In a balanced position stand with feet shoulder-width apart.

2. Knees comfortably flexed.

3. Eyes focused on the point on the ground that ball is to be bounced.

MOVING

4. Eyes remain focused on the ball.

5. Arms bend to receive the oncoming ball at waist height.

6. Distance between the hands is determined by size of ball.

7. Fingers should be spread and slightly curved as ball contacts the hands.

8. Arms give or move slightly upwards as ball contacts the hands.

9. Ball is pushed down with both hands by extending arms downwards.

10. Ball should be caught with the hands on each side of the ball.

TEACHABLE POINTS

1. Child keeps in a balanced position with the feet comfortably spaced.

2. Eyes are focused on the ball at all times.

3. Ball is pushed down with both hands by extending arms downward. (Does not "drop" the ball.)

4. Arms bend to receive oncoming ball at waist height.

5. Ball is caught at the sides with the fingers relaxed and spread (not patted).

6. When the ball meets the hands, arms bend at the elbows and cushion the impact of the ball.

BOUNCING AND CATCHING ACTIVITIES
(Large Ball)

The equipment needed for these activities are a junior-size basketball, large quality playground ball, volleyball, or soccer ball.

1. Demonstrate the action of bouncing and catching. Emphasize having fingers relaxed and spread, feet apart and balanced, and eyes on the ball.

1.

2. Stand behind child. Holding child's hands in the correct position, physically assist him or her in bouncing and catching the ball. Make sure child's feet are well positioned, arms extended, and eyes on the ball.

2.

3. Stand in front of child and gently drop the ball in front of child so it bounces high enough for him or her to catch the ball without moving feet.

3.

4. Using masking tape, mark out two 3 feet (1 m) squares on the ground, one just in front of the other. Have child stand in one of the squares, facing the square for the ball to be bounced in. Observe that child *pushes* the ball to the ground, not drops it. Ensure child's arms remain extended, fingers relaxed and spread, and eyes on ball. Insist that child catch the ball in the hands, not trap it against the body.

4.

5. As child masters the action, have him or her try to bounce and catch it in rhythm to music: "bounce-catch, bounce-catch"; bounce ball higher and catch; bounce ball lower and catch.

6. Now have child walk a few steps forward while bouncing ball, stop in place and continue bouncing ball, then again walk forward and bounce ball. Keep repeating this pattern.

6.

BOUNCE - CATCH

5.

BOUNCING AND CATCHING ACTIVITIES *(Continued)* (Large Ball)

7. As child masters #6, have him or her try to bounce the ball while continuously moving, very slowly at first, then moving faster.

6.

8. Bounce the ball to child. Observe catching action and correct as needed. Repeat, but bounce ball to the sides, then short of child.

7.

9. Bounce the ball against a wall. Tell child to let the ball bounce off the wall and once on the ground, then catch it. Use a large ball at first, then repeat with a smaller ball such as a tennis ball.

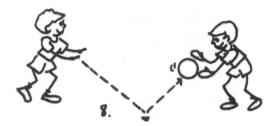

8.

10. Have child bounce the ball in two hands while kneeling on one knee; on both knees.

11. Challenge child to walk in a circle around the ball while still bouncing it on the spot with two hands. Now bounce the ball while walking in general space.

9.

12. Challenge child to keep bouncing the ball in two hands with eyes closed. Now look into different places and still keep the ball bouncing in two hands. Have child create a bouncing trick of his or her own, such as: bounce-clap, bounce-clap, bounce-clap!

10.

11.

12.

BOUNCE-CLAP!

BOUNCING CHALLENGES

1. **Obstacle Bounce.** Scatter several objects such as chairs, markers, witch's hats, ropes, hoops, and carpet mats throughout the play area. Have child bounce ball around, in and out of the obstacle course. Encourage child to look slightly ahead of the ball when bouncing it and moving through course.

2. **Scrambled Eggs-Bouncing.** Children bounce balls around each other without touching! Touched players must bounce their ball on the spot.

3. **Line Bouncing.** Have child bounce ball along a line, changing direction with the lines.

4. **Rhythm Bouncing.** Play music with a steady 4/4 beat. Have children first listen to the beat and clap its rhythm. Then have children bounce the ball with two hands in time with the rhythm. Have children make up a "ball bouncing jingle" and bounce the ball to their rhyme!

BOUNCING CHALLENGES *(Continued)*

5. *Wall Bounce.* With child, stand facing near a wall. Toss the ball at the wall and have child catch it after it bounces once off the ground. Repeat this. Offer challenges such as "clap" fingers before catching ball; "touch" shoulders before catching.

6. *Partner Wall Bounce.* Using a ball, have partners underarm throw the ball to wall, calling the name of their partner to make the catch. Start with catching the ball after one bounce off the ground, then no bounces.

7. *Bounce and Roll.* Have partners stand facing each other about 5 giant steps apart. One partner bounces the ball to the other. Receiving partner makes the catch, then rolls ball back. Reverse roles after 10 catches.

COMMON FAULTS: BOUNCING AND CATCHING WITH TWO HANDS

1. Poor stability because stance is too narrow.

2. Poor positioning of the feet and hands in relation to the oncoming ball.

3. Ball is trapped against the body.

4. Continually alters height of the body; especially bending excessively at the waist.

5. Elbows do not bend; therefore, no give with the ball to absorb force.

6. Hands and fingers are poorly shaped.

7. Too much tension in the hands and fingers.

8. Hands close too slowly or at the wrong time.

9. Ball is patted rather than caught.

10. Ball is dropped passively rather than actively bounced.

11. Not following the ball, or moving the eyes and head away at impact.

TEACHING TIPS: FIRST CORRECT THE COMPONENT THAT WILL HAVE THE GREATEST IMPACT.

☛ Practical demonstration accompanied with simple and age-appropriate instruction is important when teaching children experiencing difficulties.

☛ Constant verbal and visual feedback are essential when trying to change poor movement components. This strategy is therefore applied to each and every one of these activities.

☛ Imagery can be useful in providing cues to correct movements.

☛ Motivation is essential for maintaining attention, interest, and participation.

ACTIVITIES TO CORRECT COMMON FAULTS

1. *Poor stability because stance is too narrow.*

➤ Place foot "markers" on the ground. Have child position feet on these markers, then bounce and catch the ball.

➤ Have child move and adjust feet. Use phrases such as: "Move, Stop, and Spread."

2. *Poor positioning of the feet and hands in relation to the oncoming ball.*

➤ Stand behind child. Holding child's hands in the correct position, physically assist child in bouncing and catching the ball. Make sure child's feet are well positioned, arms extended, and eyes on the ball.

COMMON FAULTS: BOUNCING AND CATCHING WITH TWO HANDS (*Continued*)

➤ Kneel in front of child and simulate a rising ball by placing the ball on the palm and raising it upwards. Verbally instruct child when and where to move the hands. Slowly speed up the movement.

3. *Ball is trapped against the body.*

➤ (Often due to lack of confidence.) Stand behind child and, holding child's hands in the correct position, physically assist him or her in bouncing and catching the ball. Make sure child's feet are well positioned, arms extended, and eyes on the ball.

➤ Kneel in front of child and simulate a rising ball by placing the ball on the palm and raising it upwards. Verbally instruct child when and where to move the hands. Slowly speed up the movement.

➤ Verbally remind child not to pull the ball into the body.

➤ Play a game where child attempts to prevent you from tagging his or her chest by pushing the ball away with the hands.

4. *Continually alters height of the body; especially bending excessively at the waist.*

➤ Place a beanbag on child's head or shoulders and tell him or her not to let the beanbag drop off.

➤ Tell child to stand upright with arms extended and hands on the front of the thighs. Now tell child to bend from the waist until he or she feels the arms hanging loose. This is the correct position. Now ask child to slightly bend at the knees. Ask child to repeat this move until he or she gets the "feel."

➤ Verbally remind child as required.

5. *Elbows do not bend; therefore, no give with the ball to absorb force.*

➤ Explain what you want child to achieve and why. Then use verbal reminding with phrases such as "soft hands" or "giving hands."

➤ Kneel in front of child and simulate a rising ball by placing the ball on the palm and raising it upwards. Verbally instruct child when and where to move the hands. Slowly speed up the movement.

➤ Stand behind child and, holding child's hands in the correct position, physically assist him or her in bouncing and catching the ball. Call "give" each time the ball is taken.

6. *Hands and fingers are poorly shaped.*

➤ Demonstrate the bouncing action. Emphasize having hands the proper distance apart, fingers relaxed and spread, feet apart and balanced, and eyes watching the ball.

COMMON FAULTS: BOUNCING AND CATCHING WITH TWO HANDS *(Continued)*

➤ Now stand in front facing child. Have child get into the "ready stage" for catching the ball. While holding the ball very slowly, raise it towards child and observe child's actions. Emphasize eyes on ball and getting hands in the right position. Explain that the fingers move to the sides of the ball. Now have child grab the ball from your hands to get the feel of taking the ball. Again emphasize the hand position.

➤ Standing close to child, tell him or her that you are going to let go of the ball just as it reaches the level of his or her hands.

➤ Have child practice catching using a balloon.

7. *Too much tension in the hands and fingers.*

➤ Sometimes tension is inherent. Child needs to practice relaxation exercises and be trained to "feel" tension so he or she can learn to relax. Stress balls are useful for this.

➤ Verbally remind child to relax. Have child shake hands and fingers to release the tension before receiving the ball.

➤ *Imagery:* Tell child to imagine that he or she is receiving an egg and must not break it.

8. *Hands close too slowly or at the wrong time.*

➤ Play the game of Grab. Stand in front of child with a ball. If child is too slow with the hand action, try holding the ball out in front of child, balanced on your palm, with child's hands to the side of the ball. Tell child that you are going to take your hand away and drop the ball and he or she has to try and grab it before it drops.

➤ Hold the ball in front of child and have him or her try to move the hands quickly to grab it from you as you move it around.

➤ If child is too quick, use slow-moving objects such as balloons and scarves and verbally remind child not to "snatch" at the ball.

➤ Verbally remind child while bouncing the ball. Use phrases such as "quick hands" or "no snatching."

9. *Ball is patted rather than caught.*

➤ Verbally remind child to catch the sides of the ball.

➤ Stand behind child and, holding child's hands in the correct position, physically assist child in bouncing and catching the ball. Make sure child's feet are well positioned, arms extended, and eyes on the ball.

COMMON FAULTS: BOUNCING AND CATCHING WITH TWO HANDS *(Continued)*

10. *Ball is dropped passively rather than actively bounced.*

➤ Stand behind child and physically assist child to push the ball to the ground.

➤ Verbally remind child to "push" or throw the ball to ground. Exaggerate the action by telling child to try to push or throw the ball harder.

11. *Not following the ball, or moving the eyes and head away at impact.*

➤ Have child lie on his or her back and complete eye-tracking exercises using a ball on a string. It is useful to have child strike the ball intermittently to improve eye-hand coordination.

➤ Working with slow floating objects such as scarves and balloons can improve child's eye tracking.

➤ Give constant verbal reminding for child to watch the ball.

BOUNCING AND CATCHING WITH TWO HANDS

Outcome/ Appearance • Success • Consistency • Rhythm • Coordination	1. Keep in a balanced position with feet comfortably spaced.	2. Eyes focused on ball at all times.	3. Ball is pushed down with both hands by extending arms downward (does not "drop" the ball).	4. Arms bend to receive oncoming ball at waist height.	5. Ball is caught at sides, with fingers relaxed and spread (not patted).	6. When ball meets hands, arms bend at elbows and cushion impact of ball.

Equipment Required:

➤ Volleyball

➤ Masking tape

Procedure (Demonstrate the procedure as you explain):

➤ Have child stand in a 2-yard/meter square.

➤ Ask child to bounce the ball continually up to 10 consecutive bounces, catching it after each bounce. (If child cannot complete 10 bounces, encourage him or her to do as many as possible.)

➤ Tell child not to retrieve any balls that are dropped.

➤ Pause between each effort.

➤ Repeat until you have assessed all the criteria.

Outcome/Appearance:

SCORE 3   If the child consistently achieves up to 10 consecutive bounces and catches and demonstrates correct technique. **(Achieved)**

SCORE 2   If the child consistently bounces and catches the ball but the technique is still not efficient. **(Almost achieved)**

SCORE 1   If the child has difficulties bouncing and/or catching the ball. **(Not yet achieved/developed)**

Assessment of Individual Criteria (Example):

4. Arms bend to receive oncoming ball at waist height.

SCORE 3   On this movement if the arms achieve this position consistently. **(Achieved)**

SCORE 2   On this movement if the arms achieve this position, but it is inconsistent. **(Almost achieved)**

SCORE 1   On this movement if the arms fail to achieve this position. **(Not yet achieved/developed)**

Assessment Tips:

➤ Ensure the ball is correctly inflated.

➤ Ensure the surface is firm and flat.

➤ Encourage the child at all times, making the assessment as non-threatening as possible.

➤ Avoid distractions.

➤ Ensure the child experiences some success before ending the assessment.

BOUNCING AND CATCHING WITH TWO HANDS

Name	Outcome/Appearance • Success • Consistency • Rhythm • Coordination	1. Keep in a balanced position with feet comfortably spaced.	2. Eyes focused on ball at all times.	3. Ball is pushed down with both hands by extending arms downward (does not "drop" the ball).	4. Arms bend to receive oncoming ball at waist height.	5. Ball is caught at sides, with fingers relaxed and spread (not patted).	6. When ball meets hands, arms bend at elbows and cushion impact of ball.

BOUNCING A LARGE BALL WITH ONE HAND

PREPARING TO MOVE

1. In a balanced position, stand with feet shoulder-width apart, foot opposite the bouncing hand, slightly ahead of the other.

2. Knees comfortably flexed.

3. Eyes focused just ahead of the spot where ball is to be bounced.

MOVING

AERIAL VIEW

4. Eyes remain focused near the ball.

5. Fingers are relaxed and spread.

6. Finger pads are used to push the ball downward and meet the ball as it comes upward.

7. Arms straighten and bend in a "pumping-like" action.

8. When the ball meets the hands, the arm bends at the elbow and cushions the impact of the ball (not "patting" or "slapping" the ball).

9. Ball is bounced in front of and to side of the body.

TEACHABLE POINTS

1. Child stands in a balanced position with feet comfortably spread.

2. Eyes are focused on the ball. When the skill level increases, the eyes can look away from the ball.

3. Ball is pushed down with the hand by extending the arm downwards.

4. Child must be ready to receive the bouncing ball, in ready position, elbow slightly bent.

5. Fingers are curved and spread.

6. Ball is bounced in front of and to side of the body.

7. Arms give or move slightly upwards as ball contacts the hands.

BOUNCING ACTIVITIES (Large Ball)

The equipment needed for these activities are a junior-size basketball, large quality playground ball, volleyball, or soccer ball.

1. Ask child to feel the ball in his or her hands. Let only the fingers touch the ball. Close eyes and feel the ball again. Now place the ball on the floor. Feel the ball again, spread the fingers of favorite hand over the ball. Close eyes and still feel the ball.

2. From kneeling position, have child bounce the ball with favorite hand. Check that the fingers are relaxed, eyes are on the ball, and finger pads are pushing the ball downward. Let the fingers meet the ball, then push it downward again. Demonstrate first, then have child copy your actions.

3. Now tell child you are going to "play the piano" on your ball. Start with the pointer finger first and use it to bounce the ball. Then take each of the other fingers in turn: middle finger, ring finger, pinky, and finally the thumb. Now use all the fingers working together to bounce the ball.

4. Do the previous activity again, and ask child to close his or her eyes while "piano bouncing" the ball.

5. Have child return to standing position. Check that knees are comfortably bent and feet are shoulder-width apart, with foot opposite bouncing hand slightly ahead of other foot. Have child bounce ball with favorite hand in the "pocket"—formed by the feet and body. How low can child bounce the ball? Bounce the ball at belly-button height, then low again.

5. "POCKET"

BOUNCING ACTIVITIES (Large Ball) (Continued)

6. Repeat #5, but ask child not to look directly at the ball, rather just slightly ahead of the ball. Play "How Many Fingers?" (Hold up fingers, ask child to look up from the ball, and tell you how many fingers he or she can see.)

7. Now have child bounce the ball in front; to one side; to the other side. Bounce the ball in place while walking around it. Bounce the ball in place, eyes focused slightly ahead of the ball.

8. Have child move forward while bouncing the ball. Walk slowly at first, then gradually get faster. Try slide-stepping and bouncing the ball. Try jogging and bouncing the ball. Remind child to try not to watch the ball, but to look slightly ahead of the ball.

9. *Scrambled Eggs—Bouncing.* Bounce ball in and out of each other in general space. Remind children to bend their knees—stay low as they bounce their balls. Bounce ball along a line. Bounce ball in and out of markers spaced about 2 meters (6 feet) apart.

10. Repeat all the above activities with other hand.

11. Now bounce the ball from one hand to the other hand. Ball forms the letter "V" in the cross-over.

BOUNCING GAMES (Large Ball)

1. **Hoop Bounce.** Ideally one hoop and one ball per child are required. Have each child find a home space and place hoop on the floor within the play area. On your signal, child will skip, slide-step, walk, jog, hop in and out of the hoop while carrying the ball. On your number signal (e.g., "3!"), child must bounce ball that number of times inside a hoop.

2. **Circle Bounce.** Use hoops to mark out a large circle. Have each child stand behind a hoop and bounce a ball inside the hoop. On number and direction signal (e.g., "2—left!"), players roll the ball to the player on the left, then on to the next player on the left (two places), then continue to bounce the ball in the hoop, waiting for the next signal.

3. **Bounce & Shake.** Bounce the ball with one hand and use the free hand to shake hands with another player. Change bouncing hands and continue.

4. **Bounce & Touch.** Have child bounce the ball while touching the objects you name with the free hand. Change the bouncing hand, and continue the game.

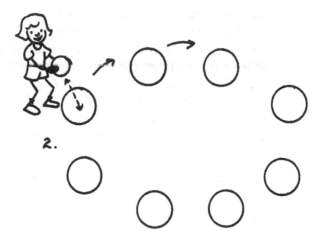

BOUNCING GAMES (Large Ball) *(Continued)*

5. ***Copy-Me Bounce.*** Have child copy your bouncing movements: bounce with right/left hand; moving forward, sideways; skipping, jumping, walking jogging; high, low; fast, slow; and so on. On your signal "Freeze!" child jump-stops and holds the ball in both hands near belly button. Take turns copying each other's bouncing actions!

5.   JOGGING

6. ***Knock-Away Bounce.*** Play this game in a small marked-out area. Each partner has a ball and starts with 10 points. Partners try to knock each other's ball away with the free hand while using the other hand to keep the ball bouncing. Child loses a point if ball is knocked away; gains a point if he or she knocks a ball away. Emphasize that players cannot touch the ball with both hands; carry the ball; or stop and hold the ball, then bounce it again.

6.

COMMON FAULTS:
BOUNCING A BALL WITH ONE HAND

1. Poor balance due to narrow stance.

2. Arm does not extend downward, but stays rigid.

3. Arm does not give slightly upward as ball contacts hands.

4. Elbow does not bend; therefore, no give with the ball to absorb force.

5. Hands and fingers are poorly shaped.

6. Ball is "patted" or slapped rather than pushed down off the fingers.

7. Too much tension in the hands, wrists, and fingers.

8. Hand closes too slowly or at the wrong time.

9. Eyes not focused on the ball or just in front of the ball.

TEACHING TIPS: FIRST CORRECT THE COMPONENT THAT WILL HAVE THE GREATEST IMPACT.

- Practical demonstration accompanied with simple and age-appropriate instruction is important when teaching children experiencing difficulties.

- Constant verbal and visual feedback are essential when trying to change poor movement components. This strategy is therefore applied to each and every one of these activities.

- Imagery can be useful in providing cues to correct movements.

- Motivation is essential for maintaining attention, interest, and participation.

ACTIVITIES TO CORRECT COMMON FAULTS

1. *Poor balance due to narrow stance.*

➤ Place foot "markers" on the ground and have child stand on these markers when bouncing the ball. Markers should be placed about child's shoulder-width apart. Have child move and adjust feet. Check for "balanced feel."

2. *Arm does not extend downward, but stays rigid.*

➤ Demonstrate the "pumping action" of the arms, then have child mimic your actions. Observe for correct movement.

➤ You may need to physically guide the arm through the pumping action. Have child close his or her eyes and "feel" the pumping action of the arm.

COMMON FAULTS:
BOUNCING A BALL WITH ONE HAND *(Continued)*

3. *Arm does not give slightly upward as ball contacts hands.*

➤ Stand behind child and hold his or her arm to show him or her how hand follows the ball upwards.

➤ Now bounce a ball and have child watch the ball as it comes upward.

➤ Have child bounce the ball, observing if hand follows the path of the ball upward, and then the fingers push the ball downward.

4. *Elbow does not bend; therefore, no give with the ball to absorb force.*

➤ Explain what you want child to achieve and why. Then use verbal reminding with phrases such as "soft hands" or "giving hands."

➤ Kneel in front of child and simulate a rising ball by placing the ball on the palm and raising it upward. Verbally instruct child when and where to move the hands. Slowly speed up the movement.

➤ Stand behind child and, holding child's hands in the correct position, physically assist him or her in bouncing and catching the ball. Call "give" each time the ball is taken.

5. *Hands and fingers are poorly shaped.*

➤ Demonstrate the bouncing action. Emphasize having fingers of bouncing hand relaxed and spread over the ball, eyes watching the ball.

➤ Have child place ball on ground in front of him or her and spread fingers over the ball. Take hand away, then spread fingers back onto the ball.

6. *Ball is "patted" or slapped rather than pushed down off the fingers.*

➤ In slow motion, show child the "pumping" action of the arm and how the fingers raise upwards to meet the ball, then push gently downwards. Have child practice this with you. You can physically take his or her hand and guide it through the action.

➤ Stand behind child and hold child's hand in the correct position. Physically assist him or her in bouncing the ball.

7. *Too much tension in the hands, wrists, and fingers.*

➤ Tension can be inherent. Child may need to practice relaxation exercises. Train the child to feel tension so that he or she learns to relax. Stress balls are useful for this.

➤ Verbally remind child to relax fingers by gently shaking the bouncing hand up and down.

➤ *Imagery:* Child closes eyes and tries to feel his or her fingers bouncing the ball in a relaxed manner.

COMMON FAULTS:
BOUNCING A BALL WITH ONE HAND *(Continued)*

8. *Hand closes too slowly or at the wrong time.*

➤ Play the game of Grab. Stand in front of the child with a ball. If child is too slow with the hand action, hold the ball out in front of child, balanced on the palm, with child's hands to the side of the ball. Tell child that you are going to take your hand away and drop the ball. Have child try to grab it before it drops.

➤ Hold the ball in front of child and have him or her try to move the hands quickly to grab it from you as you move it around.

➤ If child is too quick, use slow-moving objects such as balloons and scarves and verbally remind child not to "snatch" at the ball.

➤ Verbally remind child while bouncing the ball. Use phrases such as "quick hands" or "no snatching."

9. *Eyes not focused on the ball or just in front of the ball.*

➤ Have child work with slow floating objects such as balloons and scarves to improve child's eye-tracking ability.

➤ Place a marker just slightly ahead of where the ball contacts the floor and ask child to focus on this marker while continuing to bounce the ball.

BOUNCING A LARGE BALL

Outcome/ Appearance • Success • Consistency • Rhythm • Coordination	1. Stands in balanced position with feet comfortably spread.	2. Eyes focused on ball. When skill increases, eyes can look away from ball.	3. Pushes ball down with hand by extending arm downward.	4. Must be ready to receive bouncing ball (ready position), with elbow slightly bent.	5. Fingers curved and spread.	6. Bounces in front of and to side of body.	7. When ball meets hand, arm bends at elbow and cushions impact of ball (does not "pat" or slap ball).

Equipment Required:

➤ Basketball (size according to age)
➤ Masking tape

Procedure (Demonstrate the procedure as you explain):

➤ Have child stand in a 2-yard/meter square.
➤ Ask child to bounce the ball continually up to 10 consecutive bounces. (If child cannot complete 10 bounces, encourage him or her to do as many as possible.)
➤ Tell child not to retrieve any balls that are dropped.
➤ Pause between each effort.
➤ Repeat until you have assessed all the criteria.

Outcome/Appearance:

SCORE 3 If the child consistently achieves up to 10 consecutive bounces and demonstrates correct technique. **(Achieved)**

SCORE 2 If the child bounces consistently but the technique is still not efficient. **(Almost achieved)**

SCORE 1 If the child has difficulties bouncing. **(Not yet achieved/developed)**

Assessment of Individual Criteria (Example):

6. Bounces in front of and to side of body.

SCORE 3 On this movement if the ball is bounced in this position consistently. **(Achieved)**

SCORE 2 On this movement if the ball is bounced in this position but it is inconsistent. **(Almost achieved)**

SCORE 1 On this movement if the ball is rarely bounced in this position. **(Not yet achieved/developed)**

Assessment Tips:

➤ Ensure the ball is correctly inflated.
➤ Encourage the child at all times, making the assessment as non-threatening as possible.
➤ Avoid distractions.
➤ Ensure the child experiences some success before ending the assessment.

BOUNCING A LARGE BALL

SCORE 3: Achieved
SCORE 2: Almost achieved
SCORE 1: Not yet achieved/developed

Name	Outcome/ Appearance • Success • Consistency • Rhythm • Coordination	1. Stands in balanced position with feet comfortably spread.	2. Eyes focused on ball. When skill increases, eyes can look away from ball.	3. Pushes ball down with hand by extending arm downward.	4. Must be ready to receive bouncing ball (ready position), with elbow slightly bent.	5. Fingers curved and spread.	6. Bounces in front of and to side of body.	7. When ball meets hand, arm bends at elbow and cushions impact of ball (does not "pat" or slap ball).

CATCHING A LARGE BALL

PREPARING TO MOVE

1. Facing the thrower, stand in a balanced position, feet shoulder-width apart.

2. Knees comfortably flexed.

3. Eyes focused on the ball thrower.

MOVING

4. Feet must move to get the body in a position behind the ball.

5. Eyes are tracking the ball at all times.

6. Arms, with the elbows bent and fingers spread, must be ready to receive the oncoming ball.

7. Hands move to meet the ball.

8. Distance between the hands is determined by the size of ball.

9. Fingers should be spread and slightly curved to receive the ball.

10. Arms bend at the elbows and give when the ball meets hands.

11. Ball is caught with the hands, not the arms.

12. Fingers never point at ball; they face upwards for a high ball and downwards for a low ball.

13. Ball is caught on its sides.

TEACHABLE POINTS

1. Child is in a well balanced ready position, with elbows slightly bent and fingers curved and spread.

2. Eyes are focused on the ball.

3. Arms move to meet the ball.

4. Hands are adjusted for the size of the ball.

5. Ball is cushioned on impact.

6. Ball is caught with the hands, not the arms trapping the ball against the body.

CATCHING ACTIVITIES (Large Ball)

The equipment needed for these activities are junior-size basketballs, volleyballs, or net-balls. Gator balls (soft spongy balls) are ideal and can be purchased from sports shops, but they are expensive. As you move further away to throw the ball to the child, show him or her why it is important to have relaxed hands and fingers, and to give with the ball as it meets the hands. Throwing a ball against a hard wall and having the child watch how far the ball bounces backwards, then throwing the ball against a pillow and watching how far it bounces away, will demonstrate that if the meeting with the ball is softer, it is less likely to bounce out of the hands. It is always better to start off with relaxed throws and catches, then slowly increase the amount of force in the hands required to catch the ball.

1. Demonstrate the "catching" action your-self. Emphasize having hands the proper distance apart, fingers relaxed and spread, feet apart and balanced, and eyes watching the ball.

2. Stand facing child. Have child get into the "ready stage" for catching the ball. While holding the ball, very slowly bring it toward child and observe child's actions. Emphasize eyes on ball and getting hands in the proper position. Continue to do this, gradually increasing the speed that you bring it to him or her.

3. Now have child grab the ball from your hands to get the feel. Observe fingers relaxed and forming a "nest" about the size of the ball.

4. Standing close to the child, tell him or her that you are going to let go of the ball just before it reaches his or her hands. At this point start to tell child to catch the ball and then bring it into the body. Suggest saying, "Ready, catch."

5. Using a balloon, have child practice catching.

CATCHING ACTIVITIES (Large Ball) *(Continued)*

6. Now bounce the ball to child. Gradually increase the distance; gradually increase the speed; gradually increase both.

7. Initially, starting near child, throw the ball head-height and softly (not direct and hard) to child. Then throw the ball high; low; to the sides. Observe how child makes arm adjustments. Watch hand positioning: to catch a high ball, fingers are pointing up with thumbs closer together; for a low ball, fingers are pointing down, with little fingers closer together.

8. Throw the ball short. Emphasize that child move to ball.

9. Repeat activities 7 and 8, gradually increasing distance; gradually increasing speed; then both.

10. Have child throw and catch ball to him- or herself. How many catches in a row can child make? Start with 3, then 4, and so on to improve concentration and give purpose to task.

11. Bounce the ball to child. Vary the bounce from low bounces, to medium, to high.

12. Have child throw the ball into the air, let it bounce, then catch it.

CATCHING CHALLENGES (Large Ball)

1. ***One Step Back.*** Start 2 giant steps away from child. Throw the ball to child. Make 2 successful catches, then have child take one step away from you. If the catch is missed, take one step forward. Continue in this way.

2. ***Catching Signals.*** Have child respond to the following signals:

   ➤ Toss and catch ball while walking.

   ➤ Two-handed bounce in place.

   ➤ Roll ball along the ground, run after it, and get in front and catch it.

   ➤ Bounce ball back and forth to a partner.

3. ***Throw Copycats.*** Have partners throw the ball to each other in different ways. Receiving partner returns the ball in the same way. For example: Throw high; throw low; throw waist level; throw slowly; throw quickly; roll the ball to each other; bounce the ball to each other.

4. ***Wall Throw.*** Throw ball to wall and have child move to catch ball off wall. May be necessary at first to let ball bounce, then catch.

COMMON FAULTS:
CATCHING A LARGE BALL

1. Poor balance.

2. Poor positioning of the body and hands in relation to the oncoming ball (not behind the ball).

3. Ball is trapped against the body.

4. Arms are not extended towards the ball.

5. No bending at the elbows to absorb force.

6. Hands and fingers are poorly shaped.

7. Hands close too slowly or too quickly.

8. Too much tension in the hands and fingers before and during impact.

9. Makes no hand position adjustments according to the path of the ball.

10. Hands too wide apart to receive ball correctly.

11. Clapping at ball in an attempt to catch it.

12. Not following the ball flight, or moving the eyes and head away at impact.

TEACHING TIPS: FIRST CORRECT THE COMPONENT THAT WILL HAVE THE GREATEST IMPACT.

- Practical demonstration accompanied with simple and age-appropriate instruction is important when teaching children experiencing difficulties.
- Constant verbal and visual feedback are essential when trying to change poor movement components. This strategy is therefore applied to each and every one of these activities.
- Imagery can be useful in providing cues to correct movements.
- Motivation is essential for maintaining attention, interest, and participation.

ACTIVITIES TO CORRECT COMMON FAULTS

1. Poor balance.

➤ Place foot "markers" on the ground and have child stand on these when catching.

➤ Have child move and adjust feet. Use phrases such as: "Move, stop, and spread."

COMMON FAULTS: CATCHING A LARGE BALL *(Continued)*

2. *Poor positioning of the body and hands in relation to the oncoming ball (not behind the ball).*

   ➤ Have child move sideways to a rolled ball and try to stop it with the legs. Slowly increase the speed of the roll.

   ➤ Place 4 markers 6 feet (2 meters) in front of child with each marker spaced 3 feet (1 meter) apart. Instruct child to stand in line with the middle of the inner two markers. Tell child that when the ball comes through the middle markers, he or she does not have to move. When it is rolled through either of the side markers, child must move to that side as soon as the ball passes the markers.

   ➤ A similar result can be achieved by using masking tape to mark lanes on the ground.

   ➤ Repeat the above activities, but bounce the ball and have child move to intercept.

   ➤ Use a balloon or scarves that move slowly and allow child to move and catch.

3. *Ball is trapped against the body.*

   ➤ (Often due to lack of confidence.) Stand behind child and, holding child's hands in the correct position, physically assist him or her to catch the ball thrown by a third person. Make sure child's feet are well positioned, arms extended, and eyes on the ball.

   ➤ Use a balloon or scarf that moves slowly and allow child to move and catch.

   ➤ Verbally remind child not to pull the ball into the body.

   ➤ Play a game where child attempts to prevent you from tagging his or her chest by pushing the ball away with the hands.

   ➤ Now stand in front facing child. Have child get into the "ready stage" for catching the ball (use a soft ball). While holding the ball, very slowly bring it towards child and observe child's actions; have child grab the ball from your hands to get the feel. Gradually increase the speed as you push the ball towards child.

4. *Arms are not extended towards the ball.*

   ➤ Stand behind child. Holding child's hands in the correct position, physically assist him or her in extending the arms to catch the ball.

   ➤ Now stand in front facing child. Have child get into the "ready stage" for catching the ball (use a soft ball). While holding the ball, very slowly bring it towards child and observe child's actions. Ensure that child extends hands towards the ball as he or she grabs the ball from your hands to get the feel. Gradually increase the speed with which you push the ball towards child.

COMMON FAULTS:
CATCHING A LARGE BALL *(Continued)*

➤ Use a balloon or scarf that moves slowly and allow child to move arms and hands into the correct position and catch.

5. *No bending at the elbows to absorb force.*

➤ Explain what you want child to achieve and why. Then use verbal reminding with phrases such as "soft hands" or "giving hands."

➤ Kneel in front of child and simulate an incoming ball. Verbally instruct child when and where to move his or her hands. Push against child's hands at impact and ask child to bend the elbows at this point. Slowly speed up the movement.

➤ Stand behind child. Holding child's hands in the correct position, physically assist him or her in catching the ball. Call "give" each time the ball is taken. You can exaggerate the action by first using a balloon.

➤ *"Pumps"*: Face child with both you and child holding either side of the ball with extended arms. As you step forward, child will be forced to either bend elbows or be pushed backwards. Obviously, the first is preferable.

➤ Alternate between stepping forward and bending the elbows.

6. *Hands and fingers are poorly shaped.*

➤ Demonstrate the catching action. Emphasize having hands the correct distance apart, fingers relaxed and spread, feet apart and balanced, and eyes watching the ball.

➤ Now stand in front facing child. Have child get into the "ready stage" for catching the ball. While holding the ball, very slowly raise it towards child and observe child's actions. Emphasize eyes on ball and getting hands in the correct position. Explain fingers are up and behind for high balls (or thumbs close together); down and behind for low balls (or little fingers close together.) Now have child grab the ball from your hands to get the feel of taking the ball. Again emphasize the hand position.

➤ Standing close to child, tell him or her that you are going to let go of the ball just before it reaches his or her hands.

➤ Have child practice catching using a balloon.

7. *Hands close too slowly or too quickly.*

➤ Play the game of Grab. Stand in front of child with a ball. If child is too slow with the hand action, hold the ball out in front of child, balanced on the palm of your hands. Child holds hands near sides of the ball. Tell child that you are going to take your hand away and drop the ball. Child must try to grab the ball before it drops.

➤ Hold the ball in front of child and have him or her try to move his or her hands quickly to grab it from you as you move it around.

COMMON FAULTS:
CATCHING A LARGE BALL *(Continued)*

➤ If child is too quick, use slow-moving objects such as balloons and scarves and verbally remind child not to "snatch" at the ball.

➤ Verbally remind child while catching the ball. Use phrases such as "quick hands" or "no snatching."

8. *Too much tension in the hands and fingers before and during impact.*

➤ Sometimes tension is inherent. Child needs to practice relaxation exercises and be trained to feel tension so he or she can learn to relax. Stress balls are useful for this.

➤ Verbally remind child to relax and shake hands and fingers to release the tension before receiving the ball.

➤ *Imagery:* Tell child to imagine that he or she is receiving an egg and must not break it.

➤ Use light objects, such as balloons or scarves, that child can catch "softly." Cue words: "Soft hands."

9. *Makes no hand position adjustments according to the path of the ball.*

➤ Roll ball to child and have him or her move towards the ball.

➤ Roll ball to one side of child and have him or her practice moving to that side to position in front of the oncoming ball.

➤ Show child how to move and position in front of the ball. Have child mimic you.

➤ Toss ball to child so that he or she must move towards the oncoming ball.

10. *Hands too wide apart to receive ball correctly.*

➤ Hold ball out in front of child. Have child position hands on sides of ball. Remove ball and show child that hands are held as wide apart as the ball.

➤ Place ball on the ground and have child kneel and pick up the ball in two hands.

➤ Stand near child, holding ball out to child. Child reaches for the ball with hands correctly placed at sides. Gradually increase distance away from each other and toss ball to child.

11. *Clapping at ball in an attempt to catch it. (This is an immature stage of catching.)*

➤ Demonstrate the catching action. Emphasize having hands the correct distance apart, fingers relaxed and spread, feet apart and balanced, and eyes watching the ball.

COMMON FAULTS:
CATCHING A LARGE BALL *(Continued)*

➤ Now stand facing child. Have child get into the "ready stage" for catching the ball. While holding the ball, very slowly raise it towards child and observe child's actions. Emphasize eyes on ball and getting hands in the proper position. Explain fingers are up and behind for high balls (thumbs together); down and behind for low balls (little fingers together). Now have child grab the ball from your hands to get the feel of taking the ball. Again emphasize the hand position.

➤ Standing close to the child, tell him or her that you are going to let go of the ball just before it reaches his or her hands.

➤ Have child practice catching using a balloon.

12. *Not following the ball flight, or moving the eyes and head away at impact.*

➤ Use bright colored balls that attract attention.

➤ Use balloons or scarves that move slowly enough for child to track.

➤ Have child lie on his or her back and complete eye-tracking exercises using a ball on a string. It is useful to have child strike the ball intermittently to improve eye-hand coordination.

➤ Constant verbal reminding for child to watch the ball needs to be included in all of these exercises.

CATCHING A LARGE BALL

Outcome/ Appearance • Success • Consistency • Rhythm • Coordination	1. Well-balanced ready position (elbows slightly bent and fingers curved and spread).	2. Eyes focused on ball.	3. Arms move to meet ball.	4. Hands adjusted for size of ball.	5. Fingers face upward for a high ball; downward for a low ball.	6. Impact of ball is cushioned by bending arms at elbows.	7. Ball is caught with hands, not arms trapping ball against body.

Equipment Required:

➤ Volleyballs or Gator balls (soft sponge balls)

➤ Masking tape

Procedure (Demonstrate the procedure as you explain):

➤ Mark an area on the ground in which child should stand.

➤ Throwing position is approximately 10 feet (3 m) away.

➤ Using a volleyball, underarm throw to child both above and below his or her waist.

➤ Repeat until you have assessed all the criteria.

Outcome/Appearance:

SCORE 3   If the child consistently catches the ball demonstrating correct technique. **(Achieved)**

SCORE 2   If the child catches the ball inconsistently with most techniques correct. **(Almost achieved)**

SCORE 1   If the child regularly drops the ball and displays poor technique. **(Not yet achieved/developed)**

Assessment of Individual Criteria (Example):

7. Ball is caught with hands, not arms trapping ball against body.

SCORE 3   On this movement if the ball is caught in this position consistently. **(Achieved)**

SCORE 2   On this movement if the ball is caught correctly but it is inconsistent. **(Almost achieved)**

SCORE 1   On this movement if the ball is consistently trapped against the body. **(Not yet achieved/developed)**

Assessment Tips:

➤ Have a number of balls next to you to throw.

➤ Tell the child to ignore any dropped balls.

➤ Allow the child to pause between catches.

➤ Avoid any distractions.

➤ Ensure the child experiences some success before ending the assessment.

CATCHING A LARGE BALL

Name	Outcome/ Appearance • Success • Consistency • Rhythm • Coordination	1. Well-balanced ready position (elbows slightly bent and fingers curved and spread).	2. Eyes focused on ball.	3. Arms move to meet ball.	4. Hands adjusted for size of ball.	5. Fingers face upward for a high ball; downward for a low ball.	6. Impact of ball is cushioned by bending arms at elbows.	7. Ball is caught with hands, not arms trapping ball against body.

CATCHING A SMALL BALL

PREPARING TO MOVE

1. Stand facing the thrower in a balanced position, feet shoulder-width apart.

2. Knees comfortably flexed.

3. Eyes focused on the ball thrower.

MOVING

4. Feet move to get the body in a position behind the ball.

5. Receiver tracks the ball with the eyes at all times.

6. Arms with the elbows bent and fingers spread must be ready to receive the oncoming ball.

7. Hands move to meet the ball.

8. Distance between the hands is determined by the size of the ball.

9. Fingers should be spread and slightly curved to receive the ball.

10. When the ball meets the hands, arms bend at the elbows and give to cushion the impact.

11. Ball should be caught with hands, not arms.

12. Fingers never point at the ball; they face upward for a high ball or downward for a low ball.

13. Hands wrap around ball; not "clapping" at it.

TEACHABLE POINTS

1. Child is in a well-balanced "ready position" with elbows slightly bent and fingers curved and spread.

2. Eyes are focused on the ball.

3. Hands move to meet the ball.

4. Hands are adjusted for the size of the ball.

5. Fingers face upward for a high ball; downward for a low ball.

6. Ball is cushioned on impact.

7. Ball is caught correctly (not clapping it or trapping it against the body).

CATCHING ACTIVITIES (Small Ball)

The equipment required for these activities are small throwing objects such as tennis balls, beanbags, or soft foam balls. These can be purchased at a sport shop. Initially a round beanbag should be used because the child can get used to tracking and grasping a user-friendly object in his or her hand. Once the activities have been mastered using a beanbag, then move on to a soft small ball if possible, and finally a harder ball such as a tennis ball.

As you move further away to throw the ball to the child, show him or her why it is important to have relaxed hands and fingers and to give with the ball as it meets the hands. Throwing a ball against a hard wall and having the child watch how far the ball bounces backwards, then throwing the ball against a pillow and watching how far it bounces away, will demonstrate to the child that if he or she can make a "softer" meeting of the ball, it is less likely to bounce out of the hands.

1. Demonstrate the "catching" action. Emphasize having hands the proper distance apart, fingers relaxed and spread, feet apart and balanced, and eyes watching the beanbag.

2. Now stand in front facing child. Have child get into the "ready stage" for catching the beanbag. While holding the beanbag, very slowly bring it towards child and observe child's actions. Emphasize eyes on beanbag and getting hands in the correct position. Continue to do this, gradually increasing the speed that you bring beanbag to child.

3. Now tell child that you are going to let go of the beanbag just before it reaches child's hands. Suggest saying "Ready, catch."

4. Stand near child. Throw the beanbag to child and observe catching action. Gradually increase the distance of the throw; gradually increase the speed of the throw.

CATCHING ACTIVITIES (Small Ball) *(Continued)*

5. Starting again near child, throw high; throw low; throw to the sides. Observe how child makes arm adjustments. Watch hand-positioning: to catch a high ball, fingers are pointing up with thumbs closer together; for a low ball, fingers are pointing down, with little fingers closer together.

6. Throw the beanbag short and emphasize that child move to beanbag.

7. Repeat activities 5 and 6, and gradually increase the distance; increase the speed.

8. Now have child throw the beanbag up in the air to him- or herself and catch it. Observe for correct hand, fingers, and arm positioning. Catch beanbag high; catch beanbag low. Catch beanbag softly.

9. Have child toss the ball into the air, let it bounce once, then catch. Now toss, clap once, and catch ball; toss, clap twice, and catch a ball; touch a body part before catching ball.

10. Repeat the previous activities with a soft ball; then harder balls.

11. Now have child stand about 2 giant steps away from a wall. You toss the ball to the wall. Child tries to catch the ball after the first bounce. Remind child to track the ball from the wall, right into hands.

12. Encourage child to create a tossing/catching trick of his or her own. Emphasize that child controls toss and catch.

RELATED GAMES

1. *Catching Zingers.* Have partners, standing 4 giant steps apart, throw and catch a small ball to each other. If one partner misses a catch, then that partner goes down on one knee. If partner catches next throw, he or she can return to starting position. After one knee up and one knee down, go down on 2 knees; then on bottom to make catches. Every time a successful catch is made, partner can get into the former position until back into starting position.

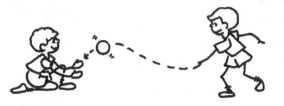

2. *Wall Game.* Have child with a partner take turns underarm tossing a ball at a wall. Mark a line so that the ball must hit above this line. Let ball bounce once before it is caught. Score one point for each successful catch.

3. *Sky Ball.* Toss the ball high into the air. Have child call "Mine!" and make the catch. Toss at a reasonable height to start and gradually toss ball higher.

RELATED GAMES *(Continued)*

4. ***Triangle Catching.*** Children, in groups of three, stand in a triangle formation, spaced about 2–3 giant steps away from each other. Partner A throws ball to Partner B, who makes the catch and then passes it to Partner C. After awhile, partners pass ball in the opposite direction: A to C to B. *Variations:* Partners pass ball to any of the other two partners. Partners must always be ready to make the catch.

5. ***Catching Tennis.*** Use a rope stretched across 2 chairs as a net. Partners stand on each side of net and underarm throw ball back and forth. Allow 1 bounce before making catch; then no bounces. Start with 2-handed catching, then just 1-hand catching.

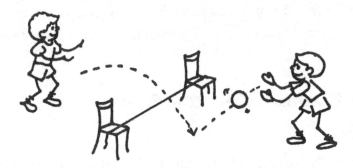

COMMON FAULTS: CATCHING A SMALL BALL

1. Poor balance.

2. Poor positioning of the body and hands in relation to the oncoming ball (not behind the ball).

3. Ball is trapped against the body.

4. Arms are not extended towards the ball.

5. No bending at the elbows to absorb force.

6. Hands and fingers are poorly shaped.

7. Hands close too slowly or too quickly.

8. Too much tension in the hands and fingers before and during impact.

9. Makes no hand position adjustments according to the path of the ball.

10. Hands too wide apart to receive ball correctly.

11. Clapping at ball in an attempt to catch it.

12. Not following the ball flight, or moving the eyes and head away at impact.

TEACHING TIPS: FIRST CORRECT THE COMPONENT THAT WILL HAVE THE GREATEST IMPACT.

☛ Practical demonstration accompanied with simple and age-appropriate instruction is important when teaching children experiencing difficulties.

☛ Constant verbal and visual feedback are essential when trying to change poor movement components. This strategy is therefore applied to each and every one of these activities.

☛ Imagery can be useful in providing cues to correct movements.

☛ Motivation is essential for maintaining attention, interest, and participation.

ACTIVITIES TO CORRECT COMMON FAULTS

1. Poor balance.

➤ Place foot markers on the ground that child must stand on when catching.

➤ Have child move and adjust feet. Use phrases such as "Move, stop, and spread."

2. Poor positioning of the body and hands in relation to the oncoming ball (not behind the ball).

➤ Have child move sideways to a rolled ball and try to stop it with the legs. Slowly increase the speed of the roll.

COMMON FAULTS:
CATCHING A SMALL BALL *(Continued)*

➤ Place 4 markers 6 feet (2 meters) in front of child, with each marker spaced 3 feet (1 meter) apart. Instruct child to stand in line with the middle of the inner two markers. Tell child that when the ball comes through the middle markers, he or she does not have to move. When it is rolled through either of the side markers, he or she must move to that side as soon as the ball passes the markers.

➤ Use masking tape to mark lanes on the ground.

➤ Repeat above activities, but bounce the ball and have child intercept.

➤ Use a balloon or scarf that moves slowly and allow child to move to catch it.

3. *Ball is trapped against the body.*

➤ (Often due to lack of confidence.) Stand behind child and, holding child's hands in the correct position, physically assist child in catching the ball thrown by a third person. Make sure child's feet are well positioned, arms extended, and eyes on the ball.

➤ Use a balloon or scarf that moves slowly and allow child to move to catch it.

➤ Verbally remind child not to pull the ball into the body.

➤ Play a game where child attempts to prevent you from tagging his or her chest by pushing the ball away with the hands.

➤ Now stand in front facing child. Have child get into the "ready stage" for catching the ball (use a soft ball). While holding the ball, very slowly bring it towards child and observe child's actions. Have child grab the ball from your hands to get the feel. Gradually increase the speed as you push the ball towards child.

4. *Arms are not extended towards the ball.*

➤ Stand behind child and, holding child's hands in the correct position, physically assist child in extending his or her arms to catch the ball.

➤ Now stand in front facing child. Have child get into the "ready stage" for catching the ball (use a soft ball). While holding the ball, very slowly bring it towards child and observe child's actions. Ensure that child extends towards the ball by grabbing the ball from your hands to get the feel. Gradually increase the speed you push the ball towards child.

➤ Use a balloon or scarf that moves slowly and allow child to move arms and hands into the correct position and catch.

5. *No bending at the elbows to absorb force.*

➤ Explain what you want child to achieve and why. Then use verbal reminding with phrases such as "soft hands" or "giving hands."

➤ Kneel in front of child and simulate an incoming ball. Verbally instruct child when and where to move his or her hands. Push against the hands at impact and ask child to bend the elbows at this point. Slowly speed up the movement.

➤ Stand behind child and, holding child's hands in the correct position, physically assist child in catching the ball. Call "give" each time the ball is taken. You can exaggerate the action by first using a balloon.

COMMON FAULTS:
CATCHING A SMALL BALL *(Continued)*

➤ *"Pumps"*: Face child with both you and child holding either side of the ball with extended arms. As you step forward, child will be forced to either bend his or her elbows or be pushed backwards. Obviously the first is preferable. Alternate between stepping forward and bending the elbows.

6. *Hands and fingers are poorly shaped.*

➤ Demonstrate the catching action. Emphasize having hands the proper distance apart, fingers relaxed and spread, feet apart and balanced, and eyes watching the ball.

➤ Now stand in front facing child. Have child get into the "ready stage" for catching the ball. While holding the ball, very slowly raise it towards child and observe child's actions. Emphasize eyes on ball and getting hands in the proper position. Explain fingers are up and behind for high balls; down and behind for low balls. Now have child grab the ball from your hands to get the "feel" of taking the ball. Again emphasize the hand position.

➤ Stand close to child. Tell him or her that you are going to let go of the ball just before it reaches child's hands.

➤ Have child practice catching a balloon.

7. *Hands close too slowly or too quickly.*

➤ Play the game of Grab. Stand in front of child with a ball. If child is too slow with his or her hand action, hold the ball out in front, balanced on the palm of your hands, with child's hands to the side of the ball. Tell child that you are going to take your hand away and drop the ball; child must try to grab the ball before it drops.

➤ Hold the ball in front of child and have child try to move his or her hands quickly to grab it from you as you move it around.

➤ If child is too quick, use slow moving objects such as balloons and scarves. Verbally remind child not to "snatch" at the ball.

➤ Verbally remind child while catching the ball. Use phrases such as "quick hands" or "no snatching."

8. *Too much tension in the hands and fingers before and during impact.*

➤ Sometimes tension is inherent. Child needs to practice relaxation exercises and be trained to feel tension so he or she can then learn to relax. Stress balls are useful for this.

➤ Verbally remind child to relax and shake hands and fingers to release tension before receiving the ball.

➤ *Imagery*: Tell child to imagine that he or she is receiving an egg and must not break it.

➤ Use light objects, such as balloons or scarves, that the child can catch "softly." Cue words: "Soft hands."

COMMON FAULTS:
CATCHING A SMALL BALL (Continued)

9. *Makes no hand position adjustments according to the path of the ball.*

   ➤ Roll ball to child and have him or her move towards the ball.

   ➤ Roll ball to one side of child and have him or her practice moving to that side to position in front of the oncoming ball.

   ➤ Show child how to move and position in front of the ball. Have child mimic you.

   ➤ Toss ball to child so that he or she must move towards the oncoming ball.

10. *Hands too wide apart to receive ball correctly.*

   ➤ Hold ball out in front of child. Have child position hands on sides of ball. Remove ball and show child that hands are held as wide apart as the ball.

   ➤ Place ball on the ground and have child kneel and pick up the ball in two hands.

   ➤ Stand near child, holding ball out to child. Child reaches for the ball with hands correctly placed at sides. Gradually increase distance away from each other and toss ball to child.

11. *Clapping at ball in an attempt to catch it. (This is an immature stage of catching.)*

   ➤ Demonstrate the catching action. Emphasize having hands the correct distance apart, fingers relaxed and spread, feet apart and balanced, and eyes watching the ball.

   ➤ Now stand in front facing child. Have child get into the "ready stage" for catching the ball. While holding the ball, very slowly raise it towards child and observe child's actions. Emphasize eyes on ball and getting hands in the proper position. Explain fingers are up and behind for high balls; down and behind for low balls. Now have child grab the ball from your hands to get the feel of taking the ball. Again emphasize the hand position.

   ➤ Standing close to the child, tell him or her that you are going to let go of the ball just before it reaches his or her hands.

   ➤ Have child practice catching using a balloon.

12. *Not following the ball flight, or moving the eyes and head away at impact.*

   ➤ Use bright colored balls that attract attention.

   ➤ Use balloons or scarves that move slowly enough for child to track.

   ➤ Have child lie on his or her back and complete eye-tracking exercises using a ball on a string. It is useful to have child strike the ball intermittently to improve eye-hand coordination.

   ➤ Constant verbal reminding for child to watch the ball needs to be included in the exercises.

CATCHING A SMALL BALL

Outcome/ Appearance • Success • Consistency • Rhythm • Coordination	1. Well-bal-anced ready position (elbows slightly bent and fingers curved and spread).	2. Eyes focused on ball.	3. Hands move to meet ball.	4. Hands adjusted for size of ball.	5. Fingers face upward for a high ball; down-ward for a low ball.	6. Cushions impact of ball.	7. Ball caught correctly (not clapping it or trapping it against body).

Equipment Required:

➤ Bucket of tennis balls

➤ Masking tape

Procedure (Demonstrate the procedure as you explain):

➤ Mark an area on the ground in which child should stand.

➤ Throwing position is approximately 3–5 meters (10–15 feet) away.

➤ Using a tennis ball, underarm throw to child both above and below his or her waist.

➤ Repeat until you have assessed all the criteria.

Outcome/Appearance:

SCORE 3   If the child consistently catches the ball demonstrating correct technique. **(Achieved)**

SCORE 2   If the child catches the ball inconsistently with most techniques correct. **(Almost achieved)**

SCORE 1   If the child regularly drops the ball and displays poor technique. **(Not yet achieved/developed)**

Assessment of Individual Criteria (Example):

5. Fingers face upward for a high ball; downward for a low ball.

SCORE 3   On this movement if the fingers achieve these positions consistently. **(Achieved)**

SCORE 2   On this movement if the fingers achieve these positions but it is inconsistent. **(Almost achieved)**

SCORE 1   On this movement if the fingers fail to achieve these positions. **(Not yet achieved/developed)**

Assessment Tips:

➤ Have a bucket of balls next to you to throw.

➤ Tell the child to ignore any dropped balls.

➤ Allow the child to pause between catches.

➤ Avoid any distractions.

➤ Ensure the child experiences some success before ending the assessment.

➤ Encourage the child at all times, thus making the assessment as non-threatening as possible.

CATCHING A SMALL BALL

SCORE 3: Achieved
SCORE 2: Almost achieved
SCORE 1: Not yet achieved/developed

Name	Outcome/ Appearance • Success • Consistency • Rhythm • Coordination	1. Well-balanced ready position (elbows slightly bent and fingers curved and spread).	2. Eyes focused on ball.	3. Hands move to meet ball.	4. Hands adjusted for size of ball.	5. Fingers face upward for a high ball; downward for a low ball.	6. Cushions impact of ball.	7. Ball caught correctly (not clapping it or trapping it against body).

UNDERHAND THROW

PREPARING TO MOVE

1. Body facing square to the target.
2. Feet placed shoulder-width apart.
3. Knees slightly flexed.
4. Ball held in the fingers.
5. Eyes focused on the target.

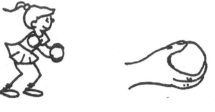

MOVING: *BACKSWING*

6. Throwing arm extends backward and downward as far as possible.
7. At the same time, weight is shifted to the foot closer to the throwing hand.

MOVING: *FORWARD*

8. Non-throwing leg steps toward the target into a diagonal position. (See diagram of feet position.)
9. Start with the hips—the shoulders will immediately follow. (This is difficult to spot; they seem to move together.)
10. Throwing arm continues toward the target in the follow-through.
11. At the completion of the throw, the weight has moved to the front foot and the rear foot is up on the toe.
12. The ball is released in front of the body.

TEACHABLE POINTS

1. Child starts in a balanced position with feet comfortably spread and faces the target.
2. Eyes are focused on the target.
3. Ball is held mainly in the fingers.
4. Weight transference occurs quickly by stepping forward with the foot opposite to the throwing arm.
5. Good arm extension in the wind-up.
6. Throw starts with the hips rotating toward the target.
7. The ball is released in front of the body (not too early or too late).
8. Good extension in the follow-through which is in the direction of the target.

UNDERHAND THROWING ACTIVITIES

Objects to be thrown include beanbags, soft small balls, and tennis balls. Concentrate on technique and then distance.

1. Using a diagonal stance with feet shoulder-width apart, have child rock back and forth, moving weight from the front foot to the back foot and back to the front.

2. As #1, but have child swing arm down and back in time with weight shifting from front to back. Count "One and two." "One" is on the way back; "and" is the pause; "two" is forward. Try to get a rhythm into the count.

3. Have child take the ball with a correct grip and stand side-on to the target. (Hold child's arm and take him or her through the action. Call: "Down as far as you can; back as far as you can; forward and throw." Repeat a number of times. Have child complete the activity without assistance, just the call.

4. Again without a ball, have child stand with feet shoulder-width apart facing the target. Now have child step forward over a line on the ground, moving weight to front foot. (Use key words "Step, swing, through.")

5. Demonstrate and have child practice the correct grip on the ball. Remember that the ball is held in the fingers.

6. Repeat activity 4 with a ball.

5. GRIP

UNDERHAND THROWING ACTIVITIES (Continued)

7. Together, throw ball back and forth. (Start close together, then gradually move away as child begins to master the task. Be aware of catching ability. If child is having some difficulty, hand or roll the ball back.)

8. To practice the follow-through, take child's hand and pull it directly towards the target. Call: "To the target." Repeat without assistance, using just the call.

9. Have child throw the ball through a hoop that you hold near him or her. Recommend using 4–5 beanbags or balls.

10. Have child throw at wall targets. Start with a large target; gradually decrease the size of target and increase the distance away. Emphasize accuracy.

11. Have child throw at set targets (cans or plastic objects). Emphasize judgment and accuracy.

12. Have child throw the ball as high as possible.

13. Have child throw to increase distance. Mark and record.

14. Have child stand in the center of a circle. You move around the circle, stop, and call for the ball. Child, at your signal, turns and throws the ball to you.

RELATED GAMES

1. ***Six Pin.*** Using 6 plastic milk bottles, set up a 6-pin bowling formation as shown. "Bowl" (roll) the ball towards the pins (milk bottles) and score a point for each bottle knocked over. *Variation:* Play Carpet Bowls. Using plastic balls, play to the rules of bowling.

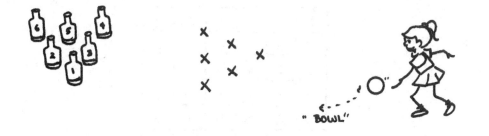

2. ***Box Toss.*** Have child toss ball or beanbag into a large cardboard box or plastic pail or bin placed near a wall. Gradually increase distance of toss. Score a point for each. *Variations:* Bounce the ball off the wall into the box. Or use a bucket filled with water and a small ball.

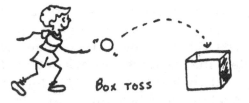

3. ***Splot! (Wall Target Tossing).*** Use chalk or carpet tape to mark out different targets on the wall. Have child toss a beanbag or soft ball at these targets. Set up a scoring system. *Variation:* Play Parent Dodge. Parent stands at wall. Child under-hand-throws ball at parent trying to hit him or her below the waist.

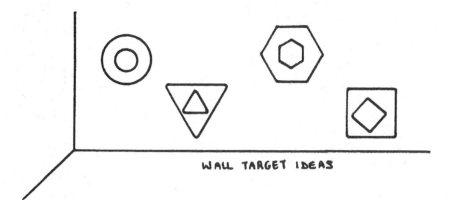

WALL TARGET IDEAS

RELATED GAMES   *(Continued)*

4. ***Grid Toss.*** Draw a grid and place numbers in the square. Have child score points according to the square hit with an underarm toss of the beanbag. *Variation:* See how many throws it takes to hit all numbers in order.

5	2	3	1	2	5
2	3	1	3	1	3
3	1	2	3	1	2
5	4	1	3	4	5
3	2	5	4	1	3
5	4	3	1	2	5

GRID TOSS

5. ***Underhand Golf.*** Together create a golf course using small balls or beanbags as the "golf ball"; hoops, rope circles, or cardboard squares as the "holes"; markers such as carpet squares as the "tee markers." Set up the course on a grassy area or a hard surface. Determine the number of holes and even the "par" (Hole 1, Par 2) for each. *Challenge:* Let child keep score of the number of throws taken to complete the course. Equal or better the score each time. Can child throw a "hole in one?"

TEE #1
OFF

HOLE ONE

PAR 3

COMMON FAULTS: UNDERHAND THROWING

1. Poor balance.

2. Incorrect foot forward.

3. Poor weight transfer in backward- and forward-throwing phases.

4. Ball held in the palm rather than fingers.

5. Arm does not extend on backward arm action.

6. Poor timing of release (too soon or too late).

7. Poor follow-through.

8. Not focusing the eyes on the target.

TEACHING TIPS: FIRST CORRECT THE COMPONENT THAT WILL HAVE THE GREATEST IMPACT.

☛ Practical demonstration accompanied with simple and age-appropriate instruction is important when teaching children experiencing difficulties.

☛ Constant verbal and visual feedback are essential when trying to change poor movement components. This strategy is therefore applied to each and every one of these activities.

☛ Imagery can be useful in providing cues to correct movements.

☛ Motivation is essential for maintaining attention, interest, and participation.

ACTIVITIES TO CORRECT COMMON FAULTS

1. Poor balance.

➤ Have child stand on feet markers that are positioned the correct width apart.

➤ Instruct child to always maintain a slight bend in the knees during the throwing action.

➤ Ensure that child does not lean too far forward with his or her upper body during the throw.

2. Incorrect foot forward.

➤ Have child stand on feet markers that are positioned the correct width apart and indicate left and right. The left and right marker colors could coincide with a similar colored tape placed on eac hoe of child.

➤ Verbally remind child to place his er left or right foot forward (depending on which hand child will use to thro he ball).

COMMON FAULTS:
UNDERHAND THROWING *(Continued)*

3. *Poor weight transfer in backward- and forward-throwing phases.*

➤ Using a diagonal stance with feet shoulder-width apart, have child rock back and forth moving weight from the front foot to the back foot and back again.

➤ As above, but have child swing arm down and back in time with weight shifting from front to back. Count "One and two." "One" is on the way back; "and" is the pause; "two" is forward. Try to get a rhythm into the count.

➤ Have child stand with feet shoulder-width apart facing the target. Now have child step forward over a line on the ground, moving weight to front foot. (Use cue words "Step, swing, through.")

4. *Ball held in the palm rather than fingers.*

➤ Demonstrate the correct grip to child and then ask child to mirror your grip.

➤ Start with child holding and throwing small objects such as marbles, golf balls, and small rolled-up pieces of paper. Experiment with hand and finger positions and use the guided discovery method to help child find the correct position.

➤ Ensure that the object child is throwing is not too big for his or her fingers to hold.

➤ Verbal cue: "Fast fingers, throw."

5. *Arm does not extend on backward arm action.*

➤ Have child swing his or her arm down and back as child shifts weight from front to back foot. Count "One and two." "One" is on the way back; "and" is the pause; "two" is forward. Verbal cue: Continue the backswing until I finish saying 'one' (stretch this out)."

➤ Have child take the ball with a correct grip and stand side-on to the target. Hold child's arm and take him or her through the action.

➤ Verbally remind child: "Down as far as you can; back as far as you can; throw." Repeat a number of times.

6. *Poor timing of release (too soon or too late).*

➤ Ensure that child has the correct grip in the fingers.

➤ Place a high cone at the position where child should release the ball.

➤ Teach child to self-correct. Show child that if the ball goes too high and short, he or she needs to hold onto the ball longer before letting go. If the ball is too short and low, then child needs to let go of the ball sooner. After each throw, help with this self-correction.

➤ Verbally remind child at the point when the ball should be released. Some anticipation on the part of the teacher is required.

COMMON FAULTS:
UNDERHAND THROWING *(Continued)*

7. *Poor follow-through.*

➤ Physically take child through the action.

➤ Have child swing arm down and back in time while shifting weight from front to back foot. Count "One and two." "One" is on the way back; "and" is the pause; "two" is forward. Verbal cue: "Continue the follow-through until I finish saying 'two'(stretch this out)."

➤ Stand in front of child and hold your hand at the correct ending position of the follow-through. Ask child to practice the follow-through and finish touching your hand. Do this initially without a ball and then with a ball.

➤ Verbally remind child: "Hand finishes pointing at the target."

8. *Not focusing the eyes on the target.*

➤ Praise child when he or she does focus on the target. "I really like the way you keep your eyes on the target."

➤ Verbally remind child: "Head up and eyes on the target."

➤ Make the target interesting to child and change it regularly to maintain motivation and concentration.

➤ Add realistic challenges and rewards for hitting the target.

UNDERHAND THROW

Outcome/ Appearance • Success • Consistency • Rhythm • Coordination	1. Starts in a balanced position with feet comfortably spread, facing target.	2. Eyes focused on target.	3. Ball held mainly in fingers.	4. Weight transference occurs quickly by stepping forward with foot opposite to throwing arm.	5. Good arm extension in wind-up.	6. Throw starts with hips rotating toward target.	7. Releases ball in front of body (not too early or too late).	8. Good extension in follow-through which is in direction of target.

Equipment Required:

➤ Bucket of tennis balls or beanbags

➤ Rope or masking tape for line

➤ Cones for a target

Procedure (Demonstrate the procedure as you explain):

➤ Have child stand behind a line.

➤ Place a target 5 yards/meters away and ask child to try and throw to this target.

➤ Allow child to pause between each effort.

➤ Repeat until you have assessed all the criteria.

Outcome/Appearance:

SCORE 3   If the throw appears well-coordinated and both distance and accuracy are consistent. **(Achieved)**

SCORE 2   If the throw appears reasonably coordinated, but distance and/or accuracy are inconsistent. **(Almost achieved)**

SCORE 1   If the throw lacks coordination and consistency. **(Not yet achieved/developed)**

Assessment of Individual Criteria (Example):

5. Good arm extension in wind-up.

SCORE 3   On this movement if the arm achieves this position the majority of the time. **(Achieved)**

SCORE 2   On this movement if the arm achieves this position but it is inconsistent. **(Almost achieved)**

SCORE 1   On this movement if the arm fails to achieve this position. **(Not yet achieved/developed)**

Assessment Tips:

➤ Encourage the child at all times, making the assessment as non-threatening as possible.

➤ Avoid distractions.

➤ Ensure the child experiences some success before ending the assessment.

➤ Have a bucket of balls and hand each ball to the child.

➤ Ensure that wind is not a factor as it may cause poor balance.

➤ If the weather is unsuitable, go indoors, if possible, and ask the child to throw at a target on a wall.

UNDERHAND THROW

Name	Outcome/ Appearance • Success • Consistency • Rhythm • Coordination	1. Starts in a balanced position with feet comfortably spread, facing target.	2. Eyes focused on target.	3. Ball held mainly in fingers.	4. Weight transference occurs quickly by stepping forward with foot opposite to throwing arm.	5. Good arm extension in wind-up.	6. Throw starts with hips rotating toward target.	7. Releases ball in front of body (not too early or too late).	8. Good extension in follow-through which is in direction of target.

OVERHAND THROW (Small Ball)

PREPARING TO MOVE

1. Body is side-on to the target, with opposite leg to throwing arm forward.
2. Feet are slightly apart.
3. Knees slightly flexed.
4. Ball held in the fingers, wrist cocked.
5. Eyes focused on the target.

MOVING: BACKSWING

6. Throwing arm extends backward and downward as far as possible.
7. At the same time the front foot is lifted, weight is shifted to the back foot.
8. Non-throwing arm points at the target.
9. At the completion of the backswing, the wrist extends backward.

MOVING: FORWARD

10. Non-throwing leg steps toward the target.
11. Hips rotate forward and the shoulders immediately follow.
12. As the arm moves forward, it bends approximately 90° at the elbow and then extends again at ball release.
13. At ball release, the wrist snaps downward.
14. Throwing arm continues toward the target and then past the non-throwing leg.
15. Finish in a balanced position with weight on the front foot and back foot up on the toes.

TEACHABLE POINTS

1. Child starts in a balanced position side-on to the target.
2. Eyes are focused on the target.
3. Ball is held at the base of the fingers.
4. Weight transference by stepping forward with foot opposite to throwing arm.
5. Good arm extension is evident.
6. Wrist is cocked at the back of the wind-up.
7. Throw starts with hips rotating toward the target and then shoulders follow.
8. As the arm moves forward, it bends approximately 90°.
9. Arm extends full again at ball release.
10. Ball is released in front of the body.
11. Wrist snaps downward.
12. Good extension in follow-through toward target, then down and past leg.

OVERHAND THROWING ACTIVITIES

Objects to be thrown include beanbags, soft small balls, and tennis balls. Concentrate on technique and then distance.

1. Using a side-on stance with feet shoulder-width apart, have child rock back and forth, moving weight from the front foot to the back foot, and back to the front. Count "One and two." "One" is on the way back; "and" is the pause; and "two" is forwards with heel of back foot coming up. Try to get a rhythm into the count.

2. As above with feet closer together, have child step to front foot. Call "One" (lift); "and" (pause); "two" (step). Have child swing arms in time to the feet movements.

3. Have child take the ball with a correct grip and stand side-on to the target. Non-throwing arm points at the target. (Hold child's arm and take through the action.) Cues: "Down as far as you can; back as far as you can; bend and throw." Repeat a number of times. Then child completes the activity without your assistance, but with cues.

4. Have child throw back and forth with you. (Start close and gradually move further away as the child begins to master the task. Be aware of catching ability. If child is experiencing difficulty in catching the ball, roll it back or hand it to him or her.)

5. To practice the follow-through, take child's hand and pull it directly toward the target and then down to his or her opposite hip. Call: "To the target and into the pocket." Complete without assistance, using just the cue words.

OVERHAND THROWING ACTIVITIES *(Continued)*

6. Throw for maximum distance. Place markers to indicate where child has initially thrown, and encourage child to throw further. Emphasize weight shift and arm extension.

7. Set up markers different distances away. Have child stand with feet shoulder-width apart, facing markers, holding ball in fingers. Child then steps side-on, feet now slightly wider than shoulder-width apart, and tries to throw ball past the marker.

8. Have child throw the ball as high as possible.

9. Have child throw ball at different speeds.

10. Have child throw at objects from different angles.

11. Have child throw a ball or beanbag at wall targets. Start with large targets; gradually decrease the size of the target.

12. Have child throw at objects such as cans or plastic objects set up on the ground or on a box or fence.

13. Have child stand in the center of a circle. You move around the circle, stop, and call for the ball. At your signal the child turns and throws the ball to you. Gradually increase distance.

RELATED GAMES

1. *Target Hit.* Place 3 plastic jugs in a pyramid shape on a ledge or bench. Have child overhand throw at target. How many jugs can you knock over in one throw?

TARGET HIT

2. *Grid Hit.* Tape a numbered grid on a wall. Have child overhand throw at numbers in grid. How many points can you score in 3 throws?

   ➤ Select a score, such as 51, and see how many throws it takes to add up to that score.

   ➤ Make a "letter" grid and throw at the letters until the word "fit," for example, has been hit.

   Variation: Vary the type of wall targets, such as "Bull's-eye Target." Or use a variety of different polygonal shapes.

A	B	C	D	E	F
G	H	I	J	K	L
M	N	O	P	Q	R
S	T	U	V	W	X
Y	Z	I	E	U	O
O	U	A	I	A	E

GRID HIT

3. *Bean the Ball.* Have child roll a ball along the ground, then run after the ball trying to hit it with beanbag.

BEAN THE BALL

4. *Wasps.* Have child chase a partner, trying to hit him or her with a soft ball or beanbag below the knees. If successful, partner becomes IT.

WASPS!

5. *Overhand Throw Game.* Have child create his or her own overhand throwing game. Give the game a name. Agree on the boundaries of the play area and the rules.

COMMON FAULTS: OVERHAND THROWING

1. Poor balance.

2. Incorrect foot forward.

3. Poor weight transfer in backward- and forward-throwing phases.

4. Ball held in the palm rather than fingers.

5. Arm does not extend on backward arm action.

6. Poor timing of release (too soon or too late).

7. Poor follow-through.

8. Not focusing the eyes on the target.

> **TEACHING TIPS: FIRST CORRECT THE COMPONENT THAT WILL HAVE THE GREATEST IMPACT.**
>
> ☛ Practical demonstration accompanied with simple and age-appropriate instruction is important when teaching children experiencing difficulties.
>
> ☛ Constant verbal and visual feedback are essential when trying to change poor movement components. This strategy is therefore applied to each and every one of these activities.
>
> ☛ Imagery can be useful in providing cues to correct movements.
>
> ☛ Motivation is essential for maintaining attention, interest, and participation.

ACTIVITIES TO CORRECT COMMON FAULTS

1. Poor balance.

➤ Have child stand on feet markers that are positioned the correct width apart.

➤ Instruct child to always maintain a slight bend in his or her knees during the throwing action.

➤ Ensure that child does not lean too far forward with the upper body during the throw.

2. Incorrect foot forward.

➤ Have child stand on feet markers that are positioned the correct width apart and indicating left and right. The left and right marker colors could coincide with a similar colored tape placed on each shoe of child.

➤ Verbally remind child to place the left or right foot forward (depending on which hand child will use to throw the ball).

COMMON FAULTS:
OVERHAND THROWING *(Continued)*

3. *Poor weight transfer in backward- and forward-throwing phases.*

➤ Using a diagonal stance with feet shoulder-width apart, have child rock back and forth moving his or her weight from the front foot to the back foot and back again.

➤ As above, but have child swing arm down and back in time with weight shifting from front to back. Count "One and two." "One" is on the way back; "and" is the pause; "two" is forwards. Try to get a rhythm into the count.

➤ Have child stand with feet shoulder-width apart facing the target. Now have child step forward over a line on the ground, moving weight to front foot. (Use cue words: "Step, swing, through.")

4. *Ball held in the palm rather than fingers.*

➤ Demonstrate the correct grip to child and then ask child to mirror your grip.

➤ Start with child holding and throwing small objects such as marbles, golf balls, and small rolled-up pieces of paper. Experiment with hand and finger positions and use the guided discovery method to help child find the correct position.

➤ Ensure the object child is throwing is not too big for his or her fingers to hold.

➤ Verbal cue: "Fast fingers, throw."

5. *Arm does not extend on backward arm action.*

➤ Have child swing his or her arm down and back as child shifts weight from front to back foot. Count "One and two." "One" is on the way back; "and" is the pause; "two" is forward. Verbal cue: Continue the backswing until I finish saying 'one' (stretch this out)."

➤ Have child take the ball with a correct grip and stand side-on to the target. Hold child's arm and take child through the action.

➤ Verbally remind child: "Down as far as you can; back as far as you can; throw." Repeat a number of times.

6. *Poor timing of release (too soon or too late).*

➤ Ensure that child has the correct grip in the fingers.

➤ Place a high cone at the position where child should release the ball.

➤ Teach child to self-correct. Show child that if the ball goes too high and short, he or she needs to hold onto the ball longer before letting go. If the ball is too short and low, then he or she needs to let go of the ball sooner. After each throw, help with this self-correction.

➤ Verbally remind child at the point when the ball should be released. Some anticipation on the part of the teacher is required.

COMMON FAULTS:
OVERHAND THROWING *(Continued)*

7. *Poor follow-through.*

➤ Physically take child through the action.

➤ Have child swing his or her arm down and back in time while shifting weight from front to back foot. Count "One and two." "One" is on the way back; "and" is the pause; "two" is forward. Verbal cue: Continue the follow-through until you finish saying 'two' (stretch this out)."

➤ Stand in front of child and hold your hand at the correct ending position of the follow-through. Ask child to practice the follow-through and finish touching your hand. Do this initially without a ball and then with a ball.

➤ Verbally remind child: "Hand finishes pointing at the target."

8. *Not focusing the eyes on the target.*

➤ Praise child when he or she does focus on the target. "I really like the way you keep your eyes on the target."

➤ Verbally remind child: "Head up and eyes on the target."

➤ Make the target interesting to child and change it regularly to maintain motivation and concentration.

➤ Add realistic challenges and rewards for hitting the target.

OVERHAND THROW (Small Ball)

Outcome/ Appearance • Success • Consistency • Rhythm • Coordination	1. Starts in a balanced position side-on to target.	2. Eyes focused on target. 3. Ball held at base of fingers.	4. Weight transference by stepping forward with foot opposite to throwing arm.	5. Good arm extension. 6. Wrist cocked at back of wind-up.	7. Throw starts with hips rotating toward target and then shoulders follow.	8. As arm moves forward, it bends approximately 90°. 9. Extends fully again at ball release.	10. Releases ball in front of body (not too early or too late). 11. Wrist snaps downward.	12. Good extension in follow-through, toward target, and then down and past leg.

Equipment Required:

➤ Bucket of tennis balls
➤ Rope or masking tape for line
➤ Cones for a target

Procedure (Demonstrate the procedure as you explain):

➤ Have child stand behind a line.
➤ Place a target area 15 yards/meters away and ask child to try and throw to or past this target.
➤ Allow child to pause between each effort.
➤ Repeat until you have assessed all the criteria.

Outcome/Appearance:

SCORE 3   If the throw appears well-coordinated and both distance and accuracy are consistent. **(Achieved)**

SCORE 2   If the throw appears reasonably coordinated; but distance and/or accuracy are inconsistent. **(Almost achieved)**

SCORE 1   If the throw lacks coordination and consistency. **(Not yet achieved/developed)**

Assessment of Individual Criteria (Example):

12. Good extension in follow-through, toward target, and then down and past leg.

SCORE 3   On this movement if the arm achieves this position consistently. **(Achieved)**

SCORE 2   On this movement if the arm achieves a consistent follow-through. **(Almost achieved)**

SCORE 1   On this movement if the arm fails to achieve a consistent follow-through. **(Not yet achieved/developed)**

Assessment Tips:

➤ Encourage the child at all times, making the assessment as non-threatening as possible.
➤ Avoid distractions.
➤ Ensure the child experiences some success before ending the assessment.
➤ Ensure that wind is not a factor as it may cause poor balance.
➤ If the weather is unsuitable, go indoors, if possible, and ask the child to throw as hard as he or she can at a target on a wall.

OVERHAND THROW
(Small Ball)

Name	Outcome/ Appearance • Success • Consistency • Rhythm • Coordination	1. Starts in a balanced position side-on to target.	2. Eyes focused on target. 3. Ball held at base of fingers.	4. Weight transference by stepping forward with foot opposite to throwing arm.	5. Good arm extension. 6. Wrist cocked at back of wind-up.	7. Throw starts with hips rotating toward target and then shoulders follow.	8. As arm moves for-ward, it bends approximate-ly 90°. 9. Extends fully again at ball release.	10. Releases ball in front of body (not too early or too late). 11. Wrist snaps down-ward.	12. Good extension in follow-through, toward target, and then down and

SINGLE-HANDED STRIKING
(Forehand) (Small Bat or Racquet)

PREPARING TO MOVE

1. Start in a square stance, in a balanced "ready position."
2. Knees slightly flexed.
3. "Shake hands" grip with racquet.
4. Eyes focused on the ball.

FEET POSITION

MOVING

5. Step to a side-on stance, feet shoulder-width apart.
6. Swing the racquet back horizontally with the arm, keeping a small amount of bend at the elbow.
7. Keep the head of the racquet slightly above the wrist; keep the wrist firm.
8. Weight is transferred to the front foot on the downswing by stepping forward.

9. Hips move first, then shoulders immediately follow as the arms swing down and forward.
10. Racquet arm and hand are in a straight line when hitting the ball.
11. Ball is contacted opposite the front foot.
12. Follow-through in the intended direction.
13. Keep the head steady and eyes focused on the ball throughout.

TEACHABLE POINTS

1. Child stands balanced with feet apart in the ready position.
2. Eyes are focused.
3. Striking hand extends backward until nearly straight.
4. Weight transfers forward by stepping into the swing with the foot opposite the striking hand.
5. Side-on hitting position is obtained.
6. Head of the racquet is kept slightly above the wrist and the wrist is held firm.
7. Forward swing starts with rotation of the hips.
8. Follow-through is in the intended direction.
9. Ball is struck opposite the front foot.

197

SINGLE-HANDED STRIKING ACTIVITIES

When learning the striking action, it is important that you provide activities that teach body position, force, control, and timing concepts.

1. Have child get into a sideways stance and move weight from the front foot to the back foot and back again on your signal.

2. Have child stand in square position or ready position, then step to the side-on position. Use signal "Ready position, lift and step."

1-2

3. Repeat #2, but add arm swing that starts with a small backswing and slowly increases. Make the action rhythmical, counting "one and two." "One" is the backswing; "and" is the pause at the top; and "two" is the downswing.

ONE   AND   TWO"

3.

4. Have child hit a balloon to him- or herself using front and back of hand.

5. Now hit a balloon with child, back and forth.

6. Put a soft ball in a stocking and suspend the stocking so that child can strike at it with the front and back of hand.

5.

7. Position a large soft ball on a witch's hat or a "tee." Have child stand side-on to the ball and strike the ball with an open hand towards a wall. Then repeat with child stepping side-on to ball.

6.

7.

SINGLE-HANDED STRIKING ACTIVITIES

(Continued)

8. Roll a large soft ball towards child and have him or her strike the ball (like playing tennis on the ground); throw a medium-sized ball in the air toward the child.

9. Now bounce a large soft ball toward child and have him or her return hit it.

10. Introduce a small, light-weighted racquet (like a ping-pong racquet) and have child hit a balloon upward using the racquet. Tell child to hold the racquet by "shaking hands" with it.

11. Have child strike the suspended ball in a stocking with the racquet.

12. Throw a large ball to child and have him or her hit the ball back to you with the racquet. Let ball bounce first, then strike at it. Start with a larger ball, then reduce size of ball as child improves striking ability.

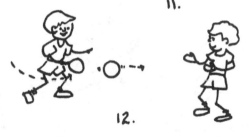

13. Repeat #12, but bounce the ball so that child has to move short distances to ball.

RELATED GAMES

1. *Partner Hit.* With a partner, have each child hold a racquet and hit a balloon back and forth. How many hits in a row can be made? Hit a ball back and forth to each other.

2. *Wall Hit.* Have child face the wall with you and hit a medium-sized soft ball with the racquet back and forth, in turn, to the wall. How many hits in a row can be made?

3. *Tennis.* Use light-weighted paddle racquets and a low net. Establish rules for hitting the ball back and forth over the net.

4. *Totem Tennis.* Suspend a ball on a long elastic rope and fix to the top of a long pole secured into the ground as shown. Have child strike the ball as it swings around. A similar product is available in toy stores or sporting stores.

COMMON FAULTS:
SINGLE-HANDED STRIKING

1. Poor balance due to a narrow stance.

2. Not standing side-on.

3. Not transferring weight.

4. Insufficient shoulder turn.

5. Getting too close to the ball; cramping the arm action.

6. Swinging upward instead of forward.

7. Bending the hitting arm excessively.

8. Dropping the wrist, or wrist too loose.

9. Poor follow-through.

10. Head moves, and/or eyes are not focused on the ball.

TEACHING TIPS: FIRST CORRECT THE COMPONENT THAT WILL HAVE THE GREATEST IMPACT.

- Practical demonstration accompanied with simple and age-appropriate instruction is important when teaching children experiencing difficulties.
- Constant verbal and visual feedback are essential when trying to change poor movement components. This strategy is therefore applied to each and every one of these activities.
- Imagery can be useful in providing cues to correct movements.
- Motivation is essential for maintaining attention, interest, and participation.

ACTIVITIES TO CORRECT COMMON FAULTS

Many of these activities should be attempted first without a ball and then with a ball.

1. Poor balance due to a narrow stance.

➤ When practicing from a stationary position, place markers on the ground to indicate where child should place his or her feet for balance. Explain why child needs to have feet apart.

➤ When stepping into a ball, 3 markers are required: 2 for the initial ready stance and 1 to indicate where the front foot should be placed.

➤ Use the cue FAST when child is taking the stance: Feet Apart, Side-on, Track ball.

COMMON FAULTS:
SINGLE-HANDED STRIKING *(Continued)*

2. *Not standing side-on.*

➤ Place markers on the ground to indicate where child should place his or her feet.

➤ Use the cue FAST when child is taking the stance: Feet Apart, Side-on, Track ball.

➤ When stepping into a ball, 3 markers are required: 2 for the initial ready stance and 1 to indicate where the front foot should be placed.

➤ Use cues such as "Chest faces the side line (or plate or marker cones placed along the side that child should face)."

3. *Not transferring weight.*

➤ With child in a sideways position, have him or her rock back and forth on the call "front back." Try to establish a rhythm.

➤ When stepping forward to meet and strike the ball, 3 markers are required: 2 for the initial ready stance and 1 to indicate where the front foot should be placed.

4. *Insufficient shoulder turn.*

➤ Have child stand in a sideways position with the racquet extended away from body in a bent-arm hitting position. Tell child not to let his or her arm move while you proceed to take the racquet backward. (The arm and shoulder move as one unit). Cue: "Turn." Repeat and establish a rhythm.

➤ Combine the above drills with a step forward. Cue: "Lift–Turn–Step."

➤ *Imagery:* Ask child to imagine his or her arm is a gate and the shoulder is the hinge. "Swing the gate."

5. *Getting too close to the ball; cramping the arm action.*

➤ Have child stand on feet markers (markers will be side-on to target and placed shoulder-width apart with front foot pointing diagonally forward). Hold ball (which child will strike) in different positions near child: too near child, too far away, suitable distance away for striking. Use a guided discovery approach for child to learn to position correctly to the oncoming ball.

➤ Stand near and face child. Toss large ball toward child so that it bounces up to striking hand (or racquet side). Child moves to correct position to strike ball.

6. *Swinging upward instead of forward.*

➤ Usually occurs when child drops the wrist and racquet head.

➤ Have child practice hitting a suspended ball that is at the height that encourages the correct racquet position.

COMMON FAULTS:
SINGLE-HANDED STRIKING *(Continued)*

➤ Ensure that child moves into a side-on position before striking the ball.

➤ Have child hold the wrist of the hitting arm with other hand, making sure child holds the wrist up which will in turn keep the racquet in the correct position.

➤ Use verbal reminding: "Keep the racquet up and swing through."

7. *Bending the hitting arm excessively.*

➤ Have child strike a ball on a string while standing on floor markers placed a correct distance away from the ball. Progress to a step and strike.

➤ Have child walk and finally run to the floor markers and strike the ball on the string.

➤ Physically take the racquet through the correct arc and ask child to feel the arm position. (Ask child to initially close his or her eyes.)

8. *Dropping the wrist, or wrist too loose.*

➤ Ensure that the racquet is not too heavy for child. You may need to instruct child to hold the handle closer to the head; if this is the case, use a lighter racquet or both.

➤ Have child practice hitting a suspended ball with his or her hand, then a small racquet. Use constant verbal reminding to keep the wrist up and firm.

➤ Have child hold the wrist of the hitting arm with his or her other hand, making sure child holds the wrist up which will in turn keep the racquet in the correct position.

9. *Poor follow-through.*

➤ *Imagery:* Ask child to imagine his or her arms continuing toward the target after he or she has struck the ball.

➤ You may need to physically take child into the correct follow-through position so that he or she can "feel it."

➤ Suspend a ball well into the follow-through path of child and ask child to strike the ball.

➤ As above, but use two balls: the first at the impact position and the second in the follow-through path.

10. *Head moves, and/or eyes are not focused on the ball.*

➤ Use bright colored balls that attract attention.

➤ Use balloons or scarves that move slowly enough for child to track.

➤ Have child lie on his or her back and complete eye-tracking exercises using a ball on a string. It is useful to have child strike the ball intermittently to improve eye-hand coordination.

➤ Constant verbal reminding for child to watch the ball needs to be included in the above exercises.

SINGLE-HANDED STRIKE (Forehand)

Outcome/ Appearance • Success • Consistency • Rhythm • Coordination	1. Balanced with feet apart (ready position).	2. Eyes focused.	3. Striking hand extends backward until nearly straight.	4. Transfer weight forward by stepping into swing with foot opposite striking hand.	5. Side-on hitting position is obtained.	6. Head of racquet is kept slightly above wrist and wrist is held firm.	7. Forward swing starts with rotation of hips.	8. Follow-through in intended direction.	9. Ball struck opposite the front foot.

Equipment Required:

➤ Bucket of balls

➤ Masking tape to indicate standing position

➤ Small paddle-type racquet

Procedure (Demonstrate the procedure as you explain):

➤ Place a line on the ground that child stands behind.

➤ The thrower stands 5–10 yards/meters away and underhand throws at waist height to child.

➤ Child is instructed to hit the ball back in the air past the thrower.

➤ Allow child to pause between each effort.

➤ Repeat until you have assessed all the criteria.

Outcome/Appearance:

SCORE 3   If the child consistently strikes the ball with control. (Achieved)

SCORE 2   If the child consistently strikes the ball but control is inconsistent. (Almost achieved)

SCORE 1   If the child has difficulty in striking the ball. (Not yet achieved/developed)

Assessment of Individual Criteria (Example):

6. Head of racquet is kept slightly above wrist and wrist is held firm.

SCORE 3   On this movement if the wrist and racquet achieve this position the majority of the time. (Achieved)

SCORE 2   On this movement if the wrist and racquet achieve this position but it is inconsistent. (Almost achieved)

SCORE 1   On this movement if the wrist and racquet fail to achieve this position. (Not yet achieved/developed)

Assessment Tips:

➤ Encourage the child at all times, making the assessment as non-threatening as possible.

➤ Avoid distractions.

➤ Ensure the child experiences some success before ending the assessment.

➤ Have a bucket of balls to throw to the child to avoid excessive delays.

➤ Ensure that wind is not a factor as hitting becomes difficult. Go inside if it is.

➤ If possible, have other children available to retrieve the balls.

SINGLE-HANDED STRIKE (Forehand)

SCORE 3: Achieved
SCORE 2: Almost achieved
SCORE 1: Not yet achieved/developed

Name	Outcome/ Appearance • Success • Consistency • Rhythm • Coordination	1. Balanced with feet apart (ready position).	2. Eyes focused.	3. Striking hand extends backward until nearly straight.	4. Transfer weight forward by stepping into swing with foot opposite striking hand.	5. Side-on hitting position is obtained.	6. Head of racquet is kept slightly above wrist and wrist is held firm.	7. Forward swing starts with rotation of hips.	8. Follow-through in intended direction.	9. Ball is struck opposite front foot.

TWO-HANDED STRIKING

PREPARING TO MOVE

1. Stance is square on; feet shoulder-width apart.

2. Knees are comfortably flexed.

3. Bat is held with the non-preferred hand closer to the end of the handle; the preferred hand is closest to the end that contacts the ball.

4. Weight is on the back foot.

5. Arms are lifted up and around the body to a point just behind the preferred shoulder with the bat facing straight up.

6. Non-preferred arm is straight but not rigid; elbow of preferred arm points to ground.

7. Head is held steady and eyes focused on ball.

MOVING

8. Knees remain flexed through the movement.

9. Weight is transferred to front foot on the downswing. (This is achieved by stepping toward the ball with front foot.)

10. Hips start the movement, and shoulders immediately follow as the arms swing down and forward.

11. At impact the hands, arms, and bat are in a straight line.

12. Ball is struck level with or slightly behind the front foot.

13. Follow-through in the intended direction and continue around the body.

14. Finish in balance position with weight on front foot; back foot is up on the toes.

TEACHABLE POINTS

1. Eyes are focused on the ball, head steady.
2. Child stands in a sideways position.
3. Weight transference occurs back and then forward (e.g., in T-Ball, by stepping into the hit).
4. Good shoulder turn in backswing.
5. Non-preferred arm remains relatively straight in backswing.
6. Hit starts with the hips rotating toward the target.
7. Knees remain flexed during the hit.
8. Good extension in the follow-through is evident.

TWO-HANDED STRIKING ACTIVITIES

To learn the striking action, it is important to provide practice activities that teach force, control, and timing.

1. Have child assume a side-on stance and shift weight from front foot to the back foot and back again on your signal.

"ONE AND TWO"

1-2.

2. Repeat #1, but add an arm swing that starts with a small action and slowly increases. Make the action rhythmical by counting "One and two": "One" is the backswing; "and" is the pause at the top; and "two" is the swing through.

3. Practice this rhythm with a small bat or rolled-up newspaper.

3.

4. Have child hit a balloon to him- or herself using front and back of the hand. Hit the balloon in different directions.

5. Using a rolled-up newspaper bound with masking tape or a light plastic bat, have child hit the balloon back and forth with you.

6. Have child swing at a large soft ball suspended in a stocking. Again practice the "One and two" rhythm.

4.   5.

7. Have child stand in side-on position and then step to hit the suspended ball. Use signal "Ready, lift, and step."

6.

TWO-HANDED STRIKING ACTIVITIES *(Continued)*

For the following activities, have the child swing from a set backswing position and then by taking a backswing.

8. Further practice this by having child hit a large light ball positioned on a tee or high cone.

9. Repeat #8 using a smaller ball.

10. Roll a large ball toward child and have him or her strike it with the bat.

11. Repeat #10 using a smaller ball.

12. Throw softly a large soft ball into the air toward the batter. Gradually reduce the size of the ball. Gradually increase the speed of your throw.

13. Have child stand side-on to a square base. Use a variety of different balls to under-hand toss toward the batter.

8.

10.

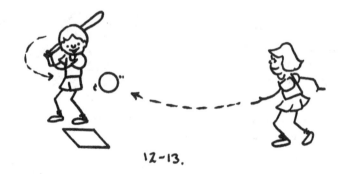

12-13.

RELATED GAMES

1. *Batting Challenge.* Give child 3 hits off a batting tee or high cone, marking how far he or she hit each time. Encourage child to equal or better the distance each time.

2. *Batter's Box.* Mark out a right angle and use 4 markers to divide this angle equally into 3 zones as shown. The batter hits off the batting tee or high cone as in the activity above, but now must select into which zone he or she will hit the ball. Batter must try to hit beyond the markers. Three fielders position beyond the markers. Have players rotate one position after every 6 hits.

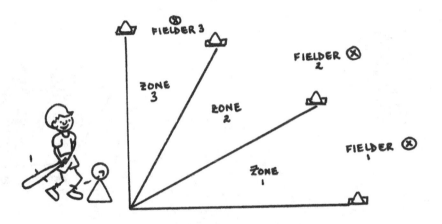

3. *Rounders.* Have child hit the ball off the batting tee, then try to run to the end zone before you can field the ball and tag him or her. If batter makes it to the end without you tagging him or her with the ball, the batter scores a point.

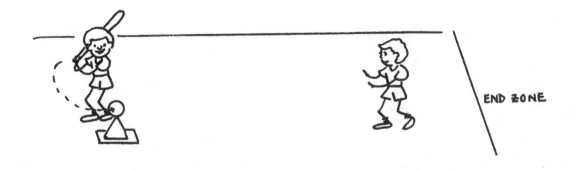

RELATED GAMES *(Continued)*

4. ***Mini-Tee Ball.*** Give each of the 3 players a role: striker, fielder, and catcher. Rotate roles after every 3 hits.

CATCHER   STRIKER   FIELDER

5. ***Continuous Cricket.*** Underarm the ball to child, who hits the ball and runs to a side marker and back to the batter's area before you can field the ball and hit the wickets. One point is scored for each successful run.

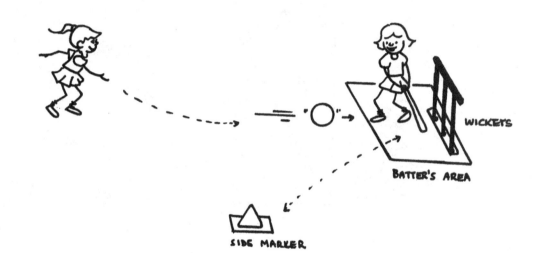

WICKETS

BATTER'S AREA

SIDE MARKER

COMMON FAULTS: TWO-HANDED STRIKING

1. Poor balance due to narrow stance or standing stiff-legged.

2. Not standing side-on.

3. Straightening the knees especially on the downswing.

4. Going up on the toes on the downswing.

5. Wrong hand position on the bat.

6. Insufficient shoulder turn.

7. Excessively bending the non-preferred arm.

8. Does not start the downswing with the hips.

9. Lack of follow-through.

10. Eyes not focused on the ball.

TEACHING TIPS: FIRST CORRECT THE COMPONENT THAT WILL HAVE THE GREATEST IMPACT.

- Practical demonstration accompanied with simple and age-appropriate instruction is important when teaching children experiencing difficulties.

- Constant verbal and visual feedback are essential when trying to change poor movement components. This strategy is therefore applied to each and every one of these activities.

- Imagery can be useful in providing cues to correct movements.

- Motivation is essential for maintaining attention, interest, and participation.

ACTIVITIES TO CORRECT COMMON FAULTS

1. *Poor balance due to narrow stance or standing stiff-legged.*

➤ To practice from a stationary position, place markers on the ground to indicate where child should place his or her feet for balance. Explain why child needs to have his or her feet apart. Introduce the concept of the "ready position."

➤ When stepping into a ball, use 3 markers: 2 for the initial ready stance and 1 to indicate where the front foot should be placed.

➤ Verbally remind child to bend knees when taking the ready stance.

2. *Not standing side-on.*

➤ Place markers on the ground to indicate where child should place his or her feet.

COMMON FAULTS:
TWO-HANDED STRIKING (Continued)

➤ Verbally remind child when taking the ready stance by using the cue word FAST: Feet Apart, Side-on, Track ball.

➤ When stepping into a ball, use 3 markers: 2 for the initial ready stance and 1 to indicate where the front foot should be placed.

➤ Verbally remind child using cues such as: "Chest faces the side line, plate, marker cones," etc.

3. Straightening the knees especially on the downswing.

➤ Use constant verbal reminding for child to keep the knees bent.

➤ Ensure that child is not moving excessively forward with the upper body.

➤ Have child complete small swings back and forth, concentrating on keeping the knees bent. Slowly increase the size of the swing.

4. Going up on the toes on the downswing.

➤ Have child place his or her weight into the heels and concentrate on keeping it there throughout the swing.

➤ Imagery: Have child imagine that he or she is in a "sitting position" which will keep the weight back.

➤ Place a wedge or another small object under the toes of child and have child swing.

5. Wrong hand position on the bat.

➤ Use constant verbal reminding for child to place the preferred hitting hand on the top of the nonhitting hand.

➤ Place different colored tape on the bat to indicate hand position on the handle and similar colored tape around the wrist of the child.

6. Insufficient shoulder turn.

➤ Imagery: Have child imagine that he or she is turning in a barrel. This will stop swaying.

➤ Use verbal cues such as "Back faces the target." In a baseball swing, the turn is restricted because the head has to be turned to face the pitcher. In a golf swing, the head can actually turn slightly away from the ball; this will enhance a shoulder turn.

➤ Flexibility exercises for the shoulders and back may need to be included into the child's program. (Refer to Section 1.)

➤ Ensure that child transfers his or her weight to the back foot during the backswing. A reverse weight shift creates a tilt and destroys shoulder turn.

➤ Have child try to turn his or her shoulders until child feels the shoulder closer to the target touch underneath the chin. Complete this exercise initially without a ball.

COMMON FAULTS:
TWO-HANDED STRIKING *(Continued)*

7. *Excessively bending the non-preferred arm.*

   ➤ Ensure that child turns his or her shoulders and does not lift the arms.

   ➤ *Imagery:* Have child imagine that he or she is pushing the hitting implement back with the non-preferred arm rather than lifting it.

   ➤ Have child hold the wrist of the non-preferred arm with the other hand and pull this arm "out and back."

8. *Does not start the downswing with the hips.*

   ➤ It is important to ensure that child starts the hit by rotating the hips. To do this, place a small hoop around child's hips. Then ask child to pantomime hitting the ball, without touching the hoop.

   ➤ *Imagery:* Ask child to imagine that he or she is swinging in a barrel and cannot touch the sides.

   ➤ Demonstrate and then give the child the cue word "Turn" as he or she reaches the top of the backswing.

   ➤ *Imagery:* Ask child to imagine that his or her hips are a door that child needs to close once he or she reaches the top of the backswing. (For a right hander, the hinge of the door is on the left hip.)

   ➤ Tell child to finish the hit with his or her hips facing the target.

   ➤ You may need to physically take child's hips through the action.

   ➤ If the hip action is correct, the shoulder action will follow.

9. *Lack of follow-through.*

   ➤ *Imagery:* Ask child to imagine that his or her arms continue toward the target after child has struck the ball.

   ➤ You may need to physically take child into the correct follow-through position so that he or she can "feel it."

   ➤ Suspend a ball well into the follow-through path of child and ask child to strike the ball.

   ➤ Repeat as above but use two balls: the first at the impact position; the second in the follow-through path.

10. *Eyes not focused on the ball.*

   ➤ Use bright colored balls that attract attention.

   ➤ Use balloons or scarves that move slowly enough for child to track.

   ➤ Have child lie on his or her back and complete eye-tracking exercises using a ball on a string. It is useful to have child strike the ball intermittently to improve eye-hand coordination.

   ➤ Use constant verbal reminding for child to watch the ball. This point needs to be emphasized in all the above exercises.

TWO-HANDED STRIKING

Outcome/ Appearance • Success • Consistency • Rhythm • Coordination	1. Eyes focused on ball.	2. Stands in a sideways position.	3. Weight transference occurs back and then forward (e.g., in T-ball, by stepping into hit).	4. Good shoulder turn in back swing.	5. Non-preferred arm remains relatively straight in back-swing.	6. Hit starts with hips rotating toward target.	7. Knees remain flexed during hit.	8. Good extension in follow-through.

Equipment Required:

➤ T-ball stand and marked batting area
➤ Baseball bat (size according to age)
➤ 5 balls
➤ 2 cones

Procedure (Demonstrate the process as you explain):

*For this activity assessment, the ball can be struck off a T-ball stand or can be hit from a pitch.

➤ Place the two cones 30 yards/meters apart and 20 yards/meters from the hitting area.
➤ Ask child to stand in the hitting area and strike the ball firmly—and, if possible, between the 2 cones.

OR

➤ Pitch the ball underhand slowly to child from 5 yards/meters, only counting those pitches that are in the legal hitting area.
➤ Ask child to strike the ball between the cones if possible.
➤ Allow child to pause between efforts.
➤ Repeat until you have assessed all the criteria.

Outcome/Appearance:

SCORE 3   If the child consistently contacts the ball and hits it between and past the markers. **(Achieved)**

SCORE 2   If the child contacts the ball, but consistently in striking and control is still not evident. **(Almost achieved)**

SCORE 1   If the child has difficulty striking the ball. **(Not yet achieved/developed)**

Assessment of Individual Criteria (Example):

2. Stands in a sideways position.

SCORE 3   On this movement if child stands in this position consistently. **(Achieved)**

SCORE 2   On this movement if child stands in this position, but does so inconsistently. **(Almost achieved)**

SCORE 1   On this movement if child fails to stand in this position. **(Not yet achieved/developed)**

Assessment Tips:

➤ Make sure the bat is not too large for the child.
➤ Do not attempt assessment on a day that is too windy as balance as well as ball flight may be affected.
➤ Encourage the child at all times, making the assessment as non-threatening as possible.
➤ Avoid distractions.
➤ Ensure the child experiences some success before ending the assessment.

TWO-HANDED STRIKING

Name	Outcome/ Appearance • Success • Consistency • Rhythm • Coordination	1. Eyes focused on ball.	2. Stands in a sideways position.	3. Weight transference occurs back and then forward (e.g., in T-ball, by stepping into hit).	4. Good shoulder turn in back swing.	5. Non-preferred arm remains relatively straight in backswing.	6. Hit starts with hips rotating toward target.	7. Knees remain flexed during hit.	8. Good extension in follow-through.

KICKING FOR DISTANCE

PREPARING TO MOVE

1. Eyes change focus between the ball and the target.

MOVING

2. Non-kicking foot steps forward, just behind and to the side of the ball.

3. Kicking leg bends at the knee at least 90° on the backswing.

4. Body leans backward just before and during contact with the ball.

5. As the kicking leg moves forward, the instep points downward and contacts the bottom of the ball. Kick with the shoelaces.

INSTEP OF FOOT

6. Kicking leg follows through toward the target.

7. Opposite arm swings forward and sideward as the kicking leg moves forward.

8. Arm opposite the kicking leg is away from the body assisting balance.

9. Head is down with eyes focused on the ball.

TEACHABLE POINTS

1. Eyes are focused on the ball.

2. Step is forward with the non-kicking foot placed close to the ball.

3. Balance is maintained throughout kicking action.

4. Adequate bending of the kicking leg's knee in backswing is evident.

5. Ball is contacted on the instep of the kicking foot.

6. Arm opposite the kicking leg moves forward during the kick.

7. A high follow-through in the direction of the target occurs.

DISTANCE KICKING ACTIVITIES

A variety of large balls can be used to develop this skill, such as beach balls, playground balls, high-density sponge balls (Gator balls), and indoor/outdoor soccer balls available from sports and toy stores.

Initially have child work on technique and then power. The key phrase is "Step, swing through."

1. Have child hold a one-legged balance with the arm opposite the kicking foot forward, and the other arm to the side. Extend the kicking leg back, then swing through.

2. Repeat but have child step to an imaginary ball and swing kicking leg through. Emphasize that the kicking foot finish by pointing toward the target on the follow-through. Observe arm positioning for balance. Repeat several times.

3. Show child that contact with the ball is made on the shoelaces (or instep). Have child practice making this contact to the ball while you hold it. Observe that kicking foot is swung forward and underneath the ball, and that eyes are focused on the ball.

4. Have child kick a stationary balloon. Observe eyes focusing on the balloon.

5. Have child kick a stationary beach ball.

6. Have child kick a stationary playground ball or soccer ball.

7. Using chalk, place 2 marks 3 meters (10 feet) apart on a wall. Have child kick a stationary ball between these 2 markings.

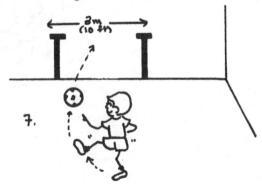

DISTANCE KICKING ACTIVITIES *(Continued)*

8. Free kick with you or partner. Gradually increase the distance.

9. Have child kick the ball as far as possible, concentrating on leaning back.

8-9.

10. Have child practice kicking the ball as high as possible. Have child concentrate on pointing the instep of the foot and looking where the contact with the ball is made.

10.

11. Repeat activities 7–10, with child approaching ball from a 3-step run-up and kicking the ball. For a right-foot kick, left foot steps first, then right, then left: "left–right–left–kick."

L   R   L   11.

12. Roll the ball slowly toward child. Have child stop the ball with the sole of the foot, then kick it.

13. Repeat #12 with child kicking the ball without first stopping it.

14. Repeat #12, then #13, with ball rolled to the side so that kicker must move into position to make the kick.

12-13.

15. Have child do the same activities as above, using the other foot.

16. Have child alternate kicking foot as he or she tries to kick between markers or goal posts.

16.

KICKING CHALLENGES

1. ***Across the Field.*** Have child kick a ball back and forth to you across a large open field. Encourage kicker to use either foot to make the kick.

2. ***Goal Kicking.*** Kick the ball through the soccer goals. Kick from different angles and different distances. As skill improves, gradually increase the distance and reduce size of goals.

KICKING GAMES

1. *Spot Kicking.* Use hoops or rope circles to designate 5 kicking spots around the goal area. Let each spot be worth so many points according to difficulty. Have one child be the kicker, the other be the retriever. Change roles after every 5 kicks. Each kicker keeps track of number of points earned each kicking round. *Variations:* Start from #1 Spot. Move to #2 Spot when a successful kick has been made from #1 Spot. Or only take one attempt from each spot to kick the ball through the goal posts. Count the number of goals scored.

2. *Kicking Golf.* Set up a fairway with a "tee-off" area and a "green." How many kicks will it take to kick the ball through the "hole"?

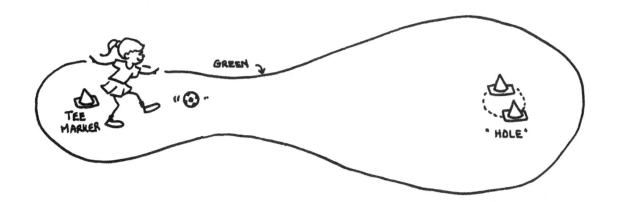

COMMON FAULTS: KICKING FOR DISTANCE

1. Poor balance.

2. Placing the non-kicking foot too close to the ball.

3. Not bending the kicking leg enough.

4. Kicking with the toe instead of instep.

5. Poor use of the opposite arm to assist balance.

6. Striking the ball off center.

7. Follow-through is incomplete.

8. Follow-through is around the body.

9. Head moves or eyes are taken off the ball.

TEACHING TIPS: FIRST CORRECT THE COMPONENT THAT WILL HAVE THE GREATEST IMPACT.

☛ Practical demonstration accompanied with simple and age-appropriate instruction is important when teaching children experiencing difficulties.

☛ Constant verbal and visual feedback are essential when trying to change poor movement components. This strategy is therefore applied to each and every one of these activities.

☛ Imagery can be useful in providing cues to correct movements.

☛ Motivation is essential for maintaining attention, interest, and participation.

ACTIVITIES TO CORRECT COMMON FAULTS

1. *Poor balance.*

➤ Practice single-leg balance activities.

➤ Hold the arm opposite the kicking leg and provide stability as child kicks from one step. Gradually decrease the amount of support.

➤ Have child take one step and support him- or herself with the arm opposite the kicking leg on your arm as he or she kicks.

2. *Placing the non-kicking foot too close to the ball.*

➤ Place a ground marker (e.g., carpet square) on the ground to indicate to child where to place the non-kicking foot.

COMMON FAULTS:
KICKING FOR DISTANCE *(Continued)*

➤ Ensure that child concentrates on having the non-kicking foot shoulder-width apart from the kicking leg.

3. *Not bending the kicking leg enough.*

➤ Flexibility exercises for the quadriceps (front thigh) and hamstring muscles may need to be completed. (Refer to Section 1.)

➤ Assist child to balance and have child hold the kicking foot behind the body and bring it slowly up to the buttock.

➤ Have child stand sideways to a wall with the kicking leg to the outside. Using the wall for balance, have child repeatedly lift kicking leg until child feels his or her foot touch your hand. Have child close his or her eyes and "feel the backswing."

4. *Kicking with the toe instead of instep.*

➤ Have child kick a balloon, which gives child enough time to concentrate on bending his or her toes down into the kicking position and striking the balloon with the instep.

➤ Have child practice leg swings with his or her ankle extended.

➤ Have child take one step, and then kick a ball suspended in a stocking just off the ground. Observe if ball is hit on the instep of foot.

➤ Have child kick a stationary ball with his or her toes pointed. Verbal cue: "Tight toes."

5. *Poor use of the opposite arm to assist balance.*

➤ Verbal cue for the arm: "Up and away."

➤ Stand to the non-kicking side of child. As child kicks, have him or her reach to the side and touch your hand.

6. *Striking the ball off center.*

➤ Have child take one step, and then kick a ball suspended in a stocking off the ground. If off center, the ball will swing to the side, providing visual feedback to child. Observe if ball is hit on the instep of foot.

➤ Repeat the above exercise but mark the ball at a point where you want child to contact it.

➤ From one step, have child kick a marked ball with the instep off a low soft tee.

➤ Have child practice kicking tennis balls off a low tee.

➤ Have child practice kicking with a marked ball indicating the contact point.

COMMON FAULTS:
KICKING FOR DISTANCE *(Continued)*

7. *Follow-through is incomplete.*

➤ Flexibility exercises for the legs may need to be introduced. (Refer to Section 1.)

➤ Strengthening exercises for the stomach muscles may be required. (Refer to Section 1.)

➤ Ensure that child can balance adequately; otherwise, he or she may find it difficult to have a high follow-through.

➤ Have child take one step, and then kick a ball suspended in a stocking off the ground. Slowly raise the height of the ball.

➤ Use a balloon so child can slow down and exaggerate the follow-through movement.

8. *Follow-through is around the body.*

➤ Have child take one step, and then kick a ball suspended in a stocking just off the ground directly in front of the body. Place a floor marker for child to place his or her non-kicking foot on and another for the foot to finish over.

➤ Use a balloon so child can slow down and exaggerate the follow-through movement.

➤ Hold your hand or a soft object in front of child and at follow-through height. Have child kick at your hand or the object.

➤ Place a line on the ground and have child keep his or her leg moving along this line.

➤ *Imagery:* Have child imagine that his or her follow-through is along a straight train track.

9. *Head moves or eyes are taken off the ball.*

➤ Use constant verbal reminding to watch the ball until contact is made.

➤ Use slow moving objects, such as balloons or scarves, to kick. These objects are excellent for tracking even though they are dropped and not kicked from the ground.

➤ Use bright colored balls for added stimulation.

➤ Other tracking exercises may be employed.

KICKING FOR DISTANCE

Outcome/ Appearance • Success • Consistency • Rhythm • Coordination	1. Eyes focused on ball.	2. Step forward with non-kicking foot (placed close to ball).	3. Balance maintained throughout kicking action.	4. Adequate bending of kicking leg's knee in backswing.	5. Ball contacted on instep of kicking foot.	6. Arm opposite kicking leg moves forward during kick.	7. High follow-through in direction of target.

Equipment Required:

➤ Large clear area (preferably grass)

➤ A number of large round balls (soccer ball preferable)

➤ A ground marker to kick from and 2 cones to kick to

Procedure (Demonstrate the process as you explain):

➤ Place the 2 cones 20 yards/meters apart and 15 yards/meters in front of the kicking point.

➤ Ask child to try to kick between and past these markers.

➤ Allow child to pause between efforts.

➤ Repeat until you have assessed all the criteria.

Outcome/Appearance:

SCORE 3   If the ball is struck consistently and both distance and accuracy are also consistent. (Achieved)

SCORE 2   If the ball is struck consistently but distance and accuracy are inconsistent. (Almost achieved)

SCORE 1   If the ball is struck consistently poorly. (Not yet achieved/developed)

Assessment of Individual Criteria (Example):

5. Ball contacted on instep of kicking foot.

SCORE 3   On this movement if the contact position is achieved consistently. (Achieved)

SCORE 2   On this movement if the contact position is achieved but it is inconsistent. (Almost achieved)

SCORE 1   On this movement if the contact position consistently fails to be achieved. (Not yet achieved/developed)

Assessment Tips:

➤ Ensure the ball is correctly inflated.

➤ Ensure the kicking area is firm, flat, and not slippery.

➤ Do not attempt assessment on a day that is too windy as balance and flight may be affected.

➤ Encourage the child at all times, making the assessment as non-threatening as possible.

➤ Avoid distractions.

➤ Ensure the child experiences some success before ending the assessment.

➤ If possible, have other children collect the balls.

KICKING FOR DISTANCE

SCORE 3: Achieved
SCORE 2: Almost achieved
SCORE 1: Not yet achieved/developed

Name	Outcome/ Appearance • Success • Consistency • Rhythm • Coordination	1. Eyes focused on ball.	2. Step forward with non-kicking foot (placed close to ball).	3. Balance maintained throughout kicking action.	4. Adequate bending of kicking leg's knee in back-swing.	5. Ball contacted on instep of kicking foot.	6. Arm opposite kicking leg moves forward during kick.	7. High follow-through in direction of target.

KICKING FOR ACCURACY

PREPARING TO MOVE

1. Head is down with eyes focused on the ball.

MOVING

2. Non-kicking foot is placed to the side of the ball.

3. Kicking foot is turned so that the inside of the foot faces the ball.

4. Kicking foot remains firm at the ankle while kicking.

5. Leg of the kicking foot is bent on the back-swing.

6. Opposite arm swings forward as the kicking leg moves forward.

7. Arm on the same side as kicking leg is away from the body assisting balance.

8. Follow-through toward the target.

9. Eyes remain focused on the ball during the movement.

INSIDE OF FOOT

TEACHABLE POINTS

1. Eyes are focused on the ball.

2. Step is into the correct position with the non-kicking foot placed close to the ball.

3. Adequate backswing of the kicking leg is evident.

4. Ball is contacted on the inside of the kicking foot.

5. Balance is maintained throughout kicking action.

6. Good extension in the follow-through in the direction of the target occurs.

ACCURACY KICKING ACTIVITIES

A variety of large balls can be used to develop this skill, such as beach balls, playground balls, high-density sponge balls (Gator balls), and indoor/outdoor soccer balls available from sports and toy stores.

Initially the focus is on technique of kicking and then accuracy.

1. Have child stand near the ball and place his or her foot on top of the ball, with heel closer to the ground. Do this with the other foot. Tell child this is how to stop the ball from rolling, and is called a "trap."

1. "TRAP!"

2. Now gently roll the ball toward child who traps the ball with one foot; traps the ball with the other foot. Repeat until child has mastered trapping the ball. This is called the "sole-of-the-foot" trap.

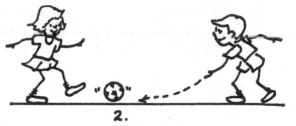

2.

3. Roll the ball slowly toward child. Have child trap the ball with the inside of the foot. Trap with ball in this way using the other foot. Gradually increase the rolling speed and have child stop the ball with the side of foot.

3.

INSIDE-OF-THE FOOT TRAP

4. Have child hold a one-legged balance with left arm forward and the right arm to the side. Extend the other foot back, then swing through.

5. Now have child push the ball with inside of his or her foot. Follow the ball. Trap it and push it again. After a while have child use the other foot to do the same activity.

4.   5.

6. Repeat but have child step to an imaginary ball and swing kicking leg through, turning the kicking foot out to the side. Emphasize that kicking foot must finish by pointing toward the target on the follow-through.

6.

ACCURACY KICKING ACTIVITIES *(Continued)*

7. Have child kick a stationary ball toward a wall. Contact with ball is made on the inside of the foot by turning the kicking foot out to the side. As the ball rebounds off the wall, have child stop (trap) the ball by using the sole of the foot or the inside of the foot. Gradually increase the distance away from the wall.

7.

8. Place 2 markers near the wall that are 3 meters (10 feet) apart. Have child kick a stationary ball between these 2 markers. Gradually increase the kicking distance.

9. Have child free kick back and forth to a partner. Gradually increase the distance. Remind child to trap ball each time before kicking.

8.

10. Repeat activities 3–5, with child approaching ball from a 3-step run-up and kicking the ball to a wall; into a wall target; to a partner. Cue words: right-foot kick; left–right–left–kick.

11. Roll the ball slowly toward and slightly to the side of child. Have child move toward the ball and stop it with the sole of the foot, then kick it back to you.

12. Repeat #11 with child kicking the ball without first stopping it.

13. Repeat the above activities using the other foot as the kicking foot.

11 – 13.

RELATED GAMES

1. ***Three-Pin Kick.*** Set up 3 plastic bottles near a wall in a triangular fashion. Have child start at a suitable distance and kick the ball to knock over targets. Gradually increase the distance. *Variation:* Use 6 plastic bottles.

2. ***Goal Kicking.*** Use witch's hats to mark out 3 meters (10 feet) goals near a wall. One partner tries to kick goals in 5 attempts; the other partner is the goalie who traps ball with his or her feet. Then change roles. Keep score.

3. ***Kicking Croquet.*** Set up markers as shown in the diagram. Ensure good spacing to allow for successful accuracy kicking. Establish a start and a finish to the course. Each successful kick must go between the markers. As skill level improves, increase the distance and reduce the space between the 2 markers.

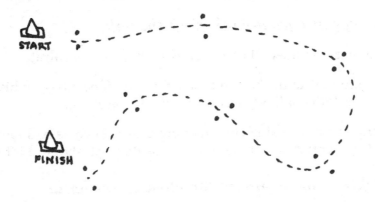

COMMON FAULTS: KICKING FOR ACCURACY

1. Head moves or eyes are taken off the ball.

2. Non-kicking foot is placed too close to the ball.

3. Not kicking with the side of the foot.

4. Poor use of the arms.

5. Striking the ball off center.

6. Follow-through is incomplete.

7. Follow-through is around the body.

> **TEACHING TIPS: FIRST CORRECT THE COMPONENT THAT WILL HAVE THE GREATEST IMPACT.**
>
> ☛ Practical demonstration accompanied with simple and age-appropriate instruction is important when teaching children experiencing difficulties.
>
> ☛ Constant verbal and visual feedback are essential when trying to change poor movement components. This strategy is therefore applied to each and every one of these activities.
>
> ☛ Imagery can be useful in providing cues to correct movements.
>
> ☛ Motivation is essential for maintaining attention, interest, and participation.

ACTIVITIES TO CORRECT COMMON FAULTS

1. *Head moves or eyes are taken off the ball.*

➤ Place a mark on the ball on which child has to concentrate.

➤ Have child look at the ball and then place a soft beanbag on his or her head. Ask child to kick the ball without dropping the beanbag.

➤ Tracking exercises using slow moving objects such as balloons and scarves are ideal. Have child kick at these objects as they are about to hit the ground.

2. *Non-kicking foot is placed too close to the ball.*

➤ Place a marker or line on the ground to indicate to child where to place his or her foot.

➤ *Imagery:* Ask child to imagine that there is a book on the ground next to the ball. Child has to place his or her non-kicking foot on the other side of this when kicking.

COMMON FAULTS:
KICKING FOR ACCURACY *(Continued)*

3. *Not kicking with the side of the foot.*

➤ Ensure that child bends the knee of the kicking leg enough to allow him or her to turn the foot outward. Some children will need to turn the toe of the non-kicking foot inward to assist this action.

➤ Have child hold a supported one-legged balance with left arm forward, and the right arm to the side (right-foot kick). Turn the kicking foot outward and extend it backward and then swing through. Repeat.

➤ Repeat but have child step to an imaginary ball and swing kicking leg through, turning the kicking foot out to the side.

➤ Use verbal cue "Crab Kick," which emphasizes that the kicking foot finish by pointing toward the target on the follow-through.

➤ Roll a ball slowly at child and have him or her stop the ball with the side of the foot. Have child then push the ball straight back with this part of the foot.

4. *Poor use of the arms.*

➤ Have child hold a supported one-legged balance with left arm forward and the right arm to the side (right-foot kick). Turn the kicking foot outward and extend it backward and then swing through. Repeat.

➤ *Imagery:* Ask child to spread his or her "wings" as he or she is kicking. Modify arm action from this point.

5. *Striking the ball off center.*

➤ Check to see if child is placing his or her body in the correct position to achieve correct contact.

➤ Have child take one step, and then kick a ball suspended in a stocking just off the ground. Observe if ball is hit on the instep of foot.

➤ As above but have child repeatedly kick the ball.

➤ Repeat the above exercise but mark the ball at a point you want child to contact with the instep.

➤ From one step, have child kick a marked ball with the instep off a low soft tee.

6. *Follow-through is incomplete.*

➤ Have child take one step, and then kick a ball suspended in a stocking just off the ground directly in front of body. Place a floor marker for child to place the non-kicking foot on and another for the foot to finish over.

COMMON FAULTS:
KICKING FOR ACCURACY *(Continued)*

➤ Use a balloon so child can slow down and exaggerate the correct follow-through movement.

➤ Hold your hand or a soft object in front of child and at follow-through height. Have child kick at your hand or the object.

➤ Place a line on the ground and have child try to keep his or her leg over the line during the follow-through.

➤ Use verbal reminding: foot finishes pointing at the target.

7. *Follow-through is around the body.*

➤ Have child take one step, and then kick a ball suspended in a stocking just off the ground directly in front of body. Place a floor marker for child to place the non-kicking foot on and another for the foot to finish over.

➤ Use a balloon so child can slow down and exaggerate the correct follow-through movement.

➤ Hold your hand or a soft object in front of child and at follow-through height. Have child kick at your hand or the object.

➤ Place a line on the ground and have child try to keep his or her leg over the line in the follow-through.

➤ Verbally remind child that his or her foot finishes by pointing at the target.

KICKING FOR ACCURACY

Outcome/ Appearance • Success • Consistency • Rhythm • Coordination	1. Eyes focused on ball.	2. Step into correct position with non-kicking foot.	3. Adequate backswing of kicking leg.	4. Ball contacted on inside of kicking foot.	5. Balance maintained throughout kicking action.	6. Good extension in follow-through in direction of target.

Equipment Required:

➤ 4 marker cones

➤ Masking tape

➤ Soccer ball (size depends upon age of child)

Procedure (Demonstrate and explain the procedure):

➤ Place 2 markers 6 feet (2 meters) apart and 10–15 feet (3–5 meters) from the marked kicking position. It is a good idea to place the markers in front of a wall.

➤ Child is instructed to kick the ball from the marked kicking position and between the middle markers if possible.

➤ Child will have as many attempts as is necessary for marking of the criteria.

➤ Allow child to pause between kicks.

Outcome/Appearance:

SCORE 3   If kick is realtively well struck, looks rhythmical, and goes consistently through the markers. **(Achieved)**

SCORE 2   If kick is relatively well struck but does not have consistency in accuracy. **(Almost achieved)**

SCORE 1   If kicking action lacks rhythm and the result is poorly struck and consistently inaccurate. **(Not yet achieved/developed)**

Assessment of Individual Criteria (Example):

2. Step into correct position with non-kicking foot.

SCORE 3   On this movement if the non-kicking foot achieves this position consistently. **(Achieved)**

SCORE 2   On this movement if the non-kicking foot achieves this position, but inconsistently. **(Almost achieved)**

SCORE 1   On this movement if the non-kicking foot fails to achieve this position. **(Not yet achieved/developed)**

Assessment Tips:

➤ Avoid having the child kick too soft or too hard as both will adversely affect the Outcome/Appearance.

➤ Provide motivation and encouragement during the assessment.

➤ Avoid distractions.

➤ Allow the child to experience some success before assessment is complete.

➤ Ensure the ball is not over- or under-inflated.

KICKING FOR ACCURACY

SCORE 3: Achieved
SCORE 2: Almost achieved
SCORE 1: Not yet achieved/developed

Name	Outcome/ Appearance • Success • Consistency • Rhythm • Coordination	1. Eyes focused on ball.	2. Step into correct position with non-kicking foot.	3. Adequate backswing of kicking leg.	4. Ball contacted on inside of kicking foot.	5. Balance maintained throughout kicking action.	6. Good extension in follow-through in direction of target.

PUNT KICKING

PREPARING TO MOVE

1. Ball is held in front of the body at hip height with both hands.
2. Fingers spread evenly diagonally across the seam of the ball.
3. Head is down with eyes focused on the ball.

MOVING

4. Kicking action starts by stepping forward onto the non-kicking foot.
5. Knee is well bent on the backswing (approximately 90°).
6. Instep is pointed downward as the leg moves forward. Ball is contacted on the instep (shoelaces).
7. Body leans backward during the downswing and contact with the ball.
8. Opposite arm swings forward as the kicking leg moves forward.
9. Hand on the side of the kicking leg guides the ball down toward the kicking foot.
10. Arm on the side of non-kicking leg is away from the body assisting balance.
11. Follow-through toward the target.

TEACHABLE POINTS

1. Eyes are focused on the ball.
2. Step is forward onto non-kicking foot.
3. Ball is held correctly in front of the body at hip height with both hands.
4. Adequate bending of the kicking leg's knee in backswing (at least 90°).
5. Ball is guided down with the hand on the same side as kicking leg (not dropped).
6. Ball is contacted on the instep of the kicking foot.
7. Arm opposite the kicking leg moves forward during the kick.
8. High follow-through occurs in the direction of the target.

PUNT KICKING ACTIVITIES

Initially activities are provided to first develop technique, then power. First use a round ball, then a football (oval-shaped).

1. Have child hold a one-legged balance with the arm on the side of the balancing leg forward, and the other arm to the side.

2. Have child practice the kicking action without a ball, using your signals: "Step, swing through."

3. Now have child practice kicking with a balloon. Observe that child contacts the balloon with the instep of his or her foot (or the shoelaces).

4. Then have child kick a stationary ball on the ground using the instep of the foot.

5. Have child take one step, and then kick a ball suspended in a stocking off the ground. Observe if ball is hit on the instep of foot.

6. From one step, have child kick a ball with the instep of the foot, off a low soft tee.

7. Now have child hold a beach ball in both hands, drop it, then kick. This is called punt kicking!

PUNT KICKING ACTIVITIES *(Continued)*

8. Repeat #7, kicking ball off one step. Use the signal "Step, swing through."

9. Repeat activities 4–7 using 3 steps.

L   R   L   SWING

9.

10. Have child take 3 steps along a line, and practice punt kicking to a large target.

11. Now have child punt kick a round ball to you or to a partner who is stationary. Gradually have partner move further away from the kicker.

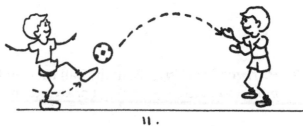

11.

12. Have child punt kick the ball for distance. Tell child the kicking leg must follow-through high and straight.

13. Have child punt kick to a moving target (you or a partner moving to the right or left of the kicker). Observe kicker's control of force and accuracy.

12.

13.

14. Practice the above activities with an oval-shaped ball.

14.

RELATED GAMES

1. ***Kick and Mark.*** One partner is the kicker; the other partner is the marker. Kicker does 3 punt kicks and marker places a beanbag where the best kick lands. Take turns.

2. ***Partner Punting.*** Punt the ball back and forth to a partner. After each successful punt and catch, take a step backward and repeat.

3. ***Goal Punting.*** Kick the ball through the goal area to score a point. How many successful kicks can be made in 5 tries?

COMMON FAULTS: PUNT KICKING

1. Not running straight at the target.

2. Not bending the kicking leg enough on the backswing.

3. Kicking with the toe instead of instep.

4. Striking the ball off center.

5. Inaccurate dropping of the ball.

6. The opposite arm not assisting in balance.

7. Follow-through is too low.

8. Follow-through is not straight, rather is around the body.

9. Ball is dropped by both hands and not guided down.

10. Head moves or eyes are taken off the ball.

TEACHING TIPS: FIRST CORRECT THE COMPONENT THAT WILL HAVE THE GREATEST IMPACT.

☛ Practical demonstration accompanied with simple and age-appropriate instruction is important when teaching children experiencing difficulties.

☛ Constant verbal and visual feedback are essential when trying to change poor movement components. This strategy is therefore applied to each and every one of these activities.

☛ Imagery can be useful in providing cues to correct movements.

☛ Motivation is essential for maintaining attention, interest, and participation.

ACTIVITIES TO CORRECT COMMON FAULTS

1. *Not running straight at the target.*

➤ Place a line on the ground and have child run in along this line.

➤ The next stage is to have child run from a single marker to a point between two markers and kick.

➤ *Imagery:* Have child imagine that he or she is running between two walls.

➤ Run closely alongside child on the side he or she usually runs to. This will prevent child from deviating to this side.

2. *Not bending the kicking leg enough on the backswing.*

➤ Flexibility exercises for the quadriceps (front thigh) and hamstring muscles may need to be completed. (Refer to Section 1.)

COMMON FAULTS: PUNT KICKING *(Continued)*

➤ Assist child to balance and have him or her hold the kicking foot behind the body and bring it slowly up to the buttocks.

➤ Have child stand sideways to a wall with the kicking leg to the outside. Using the wall for balance, have child repeatedly lift his or her kicking leg until child feels his or her foot touch your hand. Have child close his or her eyes and "feel the backswing."

3. *Kicking with the toe instead of instep.*

➤ Have child kick a balloon, which gives him or her enough time to concentrate on bending the toes down into the kicking position and striking the balloon with the instep.

➤ Have child practice leg swings with toes pointed.

➤ Have child take one step, and then kick a ball suspended in a stocking off the ground. Observe if ball is hit on the instep of foot.

➤ Have child kick a stationary ball with the toes pointed. Verbal cue: "Point the punt." Repeat this, dropping the ball.

4. *Striking the ball off center.*

➤ (Often due to incorrect ball drop.) Check that child is lowering the ball with the hand, not dropping the ball. This can be effectively taught using a balloon.

➤ Have child take one step, and then kick a ball suspended in a stocking off the ground. Observe if ball is hit on the instep of foot.

➤ Repeat the above exercise, but mark the ball at a point you want child to contact.

➤ From one step, have child kick a marked ball with the instep off a low soft tee.

➤ Now have child hold a marked beach ball in both hands, drop it, and then kick.

➤ Repeat the above activity with a normal-size ball.

5. *Inaccurate dropping of the ball.*

➤ Ensure that child runs in a straight line when kicking.

➤ Check that child is lowering the ball with the hand, not dropping the ball. This can be effectively taught using a balloon.

➤ Have child practice kicking a tennis ball. Give verbal cue to guide and lower the ball down, not drop the ball.

➤ Have child practice the first stages of the punt kick, dropping the ball on a marked point on the ground instead of kicking.

6. *The opposite arm not assisting in balance.*

➤ Give a verbal cue for the arm: "Up and away."

➤ Stand to the non-kicking side of child. As child kicks, have him or her reach to the side and touch your hand.

COMMON FAULTS: PUNT KICKING *(Continued)*

7. *Follow-through is too low.*

➤ Flexibility exercises for the legs may need to be introduced. (Refer to Section 1.)

➤ Strengthening exercises for the stomach muscles may be required. (Refer to Section 1.)

➤ Ensure that child can balance adequately; otherwise, he or she may find it difficult to have a high follow-through.

➤ Have child take one step, and then kick a ball suspended in a stocking off the ground. Slowly raise the height of the ball.

➤ Use a balloon so child can slow down and exaggerate the follow-through movement.

8. *Follow-through is not straight, rather is around the body.*

➤ Have child take one step, and then kick a ball suspended in a stocking just off the ground directly in front of the body. Place a floor marker for child to place the non-kicking foot on and another for the foot to finish over.

➤ Have child take one step, and then kick a ball suspended in a stocking just off the ground directly in front of the body.

➤ Use a balloon so child can slow down and exaggerate the correct follow-through movement.

➤ Hold your hand or a soft object in front of child and at follow-through height. Have child kick at your hand or the object.

➤ Place a line on the ground and have child try to keep his or her leg over the line during the follow-through.

➤ Verbally remind child that his or her foot should finish by pointing at the target.

9. *Ball is dropped by both hands and not guided down.*

➤ Check that child is lowering the ball with the hand, not dropping the ball. This can be effectively taught using a balloon or scarf.

➤ Have child practice kicking a small ball that can be held in one hand. Give verbal instruction to guide and lower the ball down, not drop the ball.

➤ Use the verbal cue: "Let go at the knee."

➤ Use the verbal cue: "Hang onto the ball for as long as possible."

10. *Head moves or eyes are taken off the ball.*

➤ Use constant verbal reminding for child to watch the ball until it hits the foot.

➤ Use slow moving objects, such as balloons or scarves, to kick. These objects are excellent for tracking.

➤ Use bright colored balls for added stimulation.

➤ Other tracking exercises may be employed.

PUNT KICKING

Outcome/ Appearance • Success • Consistency • Rhythm • Coordination	1. Eyes focused on ball.	2. Step forward onto non-kicking foot.	3. Ball is held correctly.	4. Adequate bending of kicking leg's knee in backswing (at least 90°).	5. Ball is guided down with hand on same side as kicking leg (not dropped).	6. Ball is contacted on instep of kicking foot.	7. Arm opposite kicking leg moves forward during kick.	8. High follow-through in direction of target.

Equipment Required:

➤ Clear open area

➤ 5 marker cones or goals

➤ 5 footballs

Procedure (Demonstrate the process as you explain):

➤ Place a cone 15 yards/meters away from the goals.

➤ Ask child to attempt to punt the ball through the goals.

➤ Allow child to pause between efforts.

➤ Repeat until you have assessed all the criteria.

Outcome/Appearance:

SCORE 3   If the ball is contacted consistently and both distance and accuracy are also consistent. **(Achieved)**

SCORE 2   If the ball is contacted consistently, but distance and accuracy are inconsistent. **(Almost achieved)**

SCORE 1   If the ball is contacted consistently poorly. **(Not yet achieved/developed)**

Assessment of Individual Criteria (Example):

6. Ball contacted on instep of kicking foot.

SCORE 3   On this movement if the contact position is achieved consistently. **(Achieved)**

SCORE 2   On this movement if the contact position is achieved, but it is inconsistent. **(Almost achieved)**

SCORE 1   On this movement if the contact position consistently fails to be achieved. **(Not yet achieved/developed)**

Assessment Tips:

➤ Ensure the ball is correctly inflated.

➤ Ensure that the kicking area is firm, flat, and not slippery.

➤ Do not attempt assessment on a day that is too windy as balance and flight may be affected.

➤ Encourage the child at all times, making the assessment as non-threatening as possible.

➤ Avoid distractions.

➤ If possible, have other children collect the balls.

PUNT KICKING

Name	Outcome/ Appearance • Success • Consistency • Rhythm • Coordination	1. Eyes focused on ball.	2. Step forward onto non-kicking foot.	3. Ball is held correctly.	4. Adequate bending of kicking leg's knee in backswing (at least 90°).	5. Ball is guided down with hand on same side as kicking leg (not dropped).	6. Ball is contacted on instep of kicking foot.	7. Arm opposite kicking leg moves forward during kick.	8. High follow-through in direction of target.

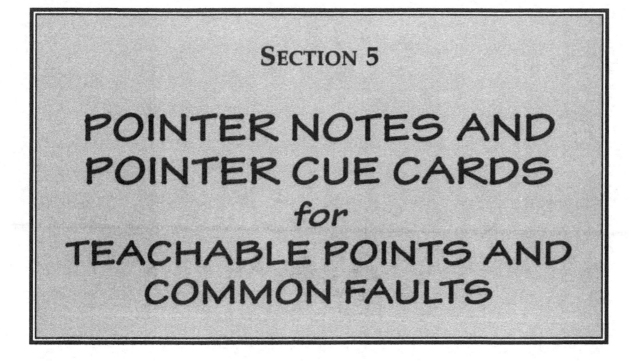

SECTION 5

POINTER NOTES AND POINTER CUE CARDS
for
TEACHABLE POINTS AND COMMON FAULTS

TEACHING FUNDAMENTAL MOVEMENT SKILLS

Fundamental movement skills are the building blocks of movement and form the foundation for skills that will be used or modified in competitive and recreational sporting activities. It is necessary that these skills are taught correctly from a young age so that incorrect movements do not become "bad habits" that are hard to change. It is also important that children succeed at these skills and develop a positive attitude toward movement and physical activity. Historically, the importance of physical activity to children in many education systems has taken a backseat to academic importance. Although many early attempts were made to link physical ability and academic achievement, it is only recently that the importance of physical competence, in its own right, has begun to be appreciated in children's development.

Physical competence affects children physically, socially, and academically, and it has a tremendous influence on a child's future development. It is, therefore, essential—from a preventative aspect—to ensure that *quality* and *quantity* of exposure to correct fundamental movement skills are necessary goals of teachers, coaches, and parents of young children.

Although the primary focus of this book is the teaching of fundamental movement skills to *young* children, the authors continually emphasize that knowledge of the correct techniques of fundamental movement skills is *essential* to teachers, coaches, and parents of children of *all* ages. As we have stated before, many of the sports skills required in games are extensions of fundamental movements.

THE MOVEMENT CONTINUUM

Fundamental movements are part of a movement continuum that commences before birth and continues for the rest of our lives. Soon after birth, an infant displays reflexes that gradually give way to essential voluntary movements that will allow the infant to socialize, explore the environment, and to literally stand on his or her own two feet.

With exposure to movement experiences, the young child begins to learn rudimentary fundamental movement skills that will hopefully be refined through good modeling, quality instruction, and opportunity to practice. Although children will reach different levels of competence, they move through similar phases.

This book can offer points of technique and some developmental teaching strategies. However, experience is the best teacher and only comes through perseverance and practice. The rewards of seeing that small boy finally being able to hit that ball or the young girl mastering her first skips because of your teaching makes the effort so worthwhile!

THE HIERARCHY OF MOTOR LEARNING

To follow is a simplified description of the hierarchy of motor learning. This concept can be used globally where each stage can be applied to the outcome of a skill, i.e., *Was the throw successful?* Alternatively, the model may be applied to elements of a skill, i.e., *Did the arm move through the correct pattern?*

For *most* skills one level is not distinct from the others and not all children necessarily achieve all stages in all activities simultaneously. For many children, when performing an activity, there exists an overlap across the stages depending on the complexity of the skill. If, for example, we take a *forward roll*, a child may *automatically* tuck his or her head when he or she commences a forward roll (stage 4), but has to *consciously think* of where to place his or her hands (stage 3) and know he or she cannot remain tucked long enough to complete the roll (stage 2). Thus it becomes obvious that there are *key* elements to any skill that have to be mastered to *at least* stage 3 before the skill can be successfully and repetitively completed.

It is an unfortunate fact that children focus on feedback relating predominantly to the outcome of their performance. *Was it successful or not?* Even though they may perform aspects of the skill correctly, they perceive the movement as a failure and react accordingly. Some children will be determined to improve, some will become frustrated, and some fear the idea of failure and may display avoidance behavior. It is, therefore, important that the parent, teacher, or coach not only assess and teach the unsuccessful elements, but encourage and provide positive feedback on those elements that the child completed correctly. Common sense tells us that if this does not occur, then self-esteem may eventually be negatively affected.

What must also be realized is that a child can be taken from stage 2 to stage 3 either by the instructor creating a need based on caring, encouragement and support, or through imposing a fear to perform correctly, based on unrealistic goals, ridicule, and enforcement. Although the short-term outcomes are similar in that the child will learn and perform the skill, the first method ensures that the child will *want* to continue learning and participating in physical activity because he or she finds it rewarding and enjoyable. The second method will most likely lead to little enjoyment and long-term avoidance of activity, especially if the enforcement is withdrawn.

"I liked the way you held the ball in your fingers!"

HIERARCHY OF MOTOR LEARNING STAGES

STAGE 1: UNKNOWING INABILITY OR ABILITY

At this stage the child has not attempted a task and, therefore, does not appreciate the skills that are necessary to successfully complete the task. If the skill is simple, then the child may perform the activity to a reasonable level and move directly to stage 3. However, if the task is difficult, success will probably elude the child and he or she will enter stage 2 of motor development.

STAGE 2: KNOWING INABILITY

This is a stage that many uncoordinated children do not progress past. If a child continues at this level, it may lead to self-esteem problems. At this stage the child is aware that the task has certain skill requirements and that his or her present level of development does not allow him or her to perform the movement successfully. How difficult the child perceives the task in relation to his or her own skill level, combined with past successes and failures, will determine whether he or she will continue to pursue the activity or avoid it. Fear of physical injury or failure will also prevent some children from progressing to stage 3.

STAGE 3: CONSCIOUS ABILITY

Children at this stage perform the task with varying degrees of success and have to consciously think of particular aspects of the movement. During this stage, as the simpler movements of the skill are mastered, they become automatic and enter stage 4. Therefore, as a child progresses through this stage, less thought will have to consciously occur during the movement and consequently, stages 3 and 4 begin to overlap.

STAGE 4: UNCONSCIOUS ABILITY

At this stage the skill no longer occupies conscious thought processes, but is automatic. It is at this level that the child is able to successfully perform other tasks at the same time. The child can perceive and react to the position of other players, concentrate on game rules and strategies, and combine smoothly series of movements.

Optimizing the teaching of fundamental movements requires the instructor to be efficient at observing movement. Observation of movement can focus on the whole skill or parts of a skill. Both methods require a sound knowledge of the correct techniques of movement. The second of these observational skills is easily obtainable when teaching young children because only one or two key points of a skill should be taught in any single session. The instructor can, therefore, make him- or herself familiar with the relevant parts of a movement before it has to be taught, or simply use pointer cards given in this book.

Global observational skills cannot be gained so quickly. To become efficient at observing movement at this level will realistically take time. In saying this, however, if the instructor is inexperienced in teaching movement, he or she can still achieve positive results by breaking down the skill to be taught into parts, imagining what a good movement looks like and concentrating only on those parts that are being taught. Eventually the ability to observe more parts of a movement and to identify poor movements will improve.

With quality instruction being given from a young age, not only will we see a significant reduction in the number of children with movement difficulties and children opting out of physical activities, but equally as important, we will see the benefits of correct technique training on the performances of even the most coordinated children.

LIFESTYLE CONSEQUENCES OF MOVEMENT

A child with motor learning difficulties is regarded as "clumsy," "awkward," or "inept." The World Health Organization has recognized motor learning difficulties as a disability, and has labeled this condition Developmental Coordination Disorder (DCD).

> **What is DCD? Performance of motor skills is substantially below that expected given the child's age and affects activities of daily living and/or academic performance. The inefficient movement is not due to a diagnosed medical or physical disorder. Other acceptable terms synonymous with DCD are "motor impairment," "inefficient movement," "movement dysfunction," and "motor learning disability."**

Movement is essential to the normal development of children and should not be ignored. Children require a variety of movement experiences through play opportunities and quality instruction. A child experiencing motor difficulties from an early age may experience negative effects in other areas of his or her development.

Children are active learners and need to move to learn and at the same time learn to move.

Physical stimulation and education at home, in schools, and sporting clubs offer children the benefits of improved coordination and motor fitness (endurance, strength, flexibility, etc.) that has lifestyle benefits now and for the future. Improved motor coordination increases the child's ability to participate successfully and with confidence in a variety of play, sporting, and recreational opportunities that are available. Physical games, modified or traditional, provide an interesting and safe environment in which to learn social skills such as positive interaction, communication, sharing, acceptance, and tolerance of one's own and other people's strengths and weaknesses.

For the uncoordinated child in the home and school environment, there is the danger of negative social aspects such as ridicule, exclusion, and loss of self-esteem. Statements such as "He'll grow out of it" or "She's just going through an awkward time" are generally incorrect. Many children do not outgrow coordination problems or cease being awkward. What does happen is that they are exposed to a physical and psychological risk that may affect them for the rest of their lives. Indeed, offering explanations such as those mentioned above has been an excuse for neglect over what is a potentially harmful situation. Being uncoordinated can affect a child's life more than just having difficulties with sports or being unfit.

The immediate problem that an uncoordinated child faces is that of ridicule and damage to his or her self-esteem. Children entering our education system as a group of five-year-olds generally experience less self-esteem problems than children completing year one as six-year-olds. *Why?* Physical aspects that the year one children see as "shoulds" (things that they can't yet do but other children can) such as catching, skipping, or handling blocks, can cause them to view themselves in a negative way. The problem is highlighted because we cannot hide the way we move. Our movements are on display for all to see!

Children experiencing movement difficulties spend more time concentrating on manual tasks. This means that their minds are occupied with consciously thinking about movements rather than attending to other aspects of learning (Diagram 1).

Diagram 1
ATTENTIONAL SPACE MODEL

← **Amount of space used for different tasks** →

automatic task   semi-learned task   new task

Using this model, let's assume that a young child is attempting a new concept while practicing on a previously learned skill. For example:

> **SKILL**   *Ball bouncing*
> **CONCEPT**   *Walking around objects*

Let us also assume that this child has a coordination difficulty.

This much space is required to concentrate on what the hands are doing   *This much space to concentrate on the concept*   *This is the available space left*

But if the child was coordinated, the amount of available space in our model would appear like this.

Manual task   *Concept*   *Available space*

Now consider the teacher beginning to add another concept or strategy at this point and there is some unwanted environmental stimuli.

Needs this much space for the new instructions

But this is the present scenario of our student:

Space for manual task   Concept space   Available space for instruction

Task not grasped sufficiently for learning

Attention to unwanted stimuli

This illustrates that far too much space is being used to recall and concentrate on the movement.

Diagram 1
ATTENTIONAL SPACE MODEL *(Continued)*

If our child was coordinated, this would be the scenario:

Manual task	*Concept*	*Unwanted stimuli*	*Available space*

| | | | The task is attended to and learned |

In the previous illustration, the amount of space taken by the automated motor task is small, leaving enough available space for the child to attend to the new task successfully.

This model can be applied to a child trying to progress to the higher stages of a motor skill or play a game before the previous levels have been mastered. The result can be frustrating for the child and the teacher or parent. It is important to remember that the child can only handle so much information and the more automated the movements are, the more space available to handle new skill and game concepts.

Research has shown that often uncoordinated children do not reach their academic potential, most likely due to self-esteem problems that carry over into other learning areas. Be aware, however, of claims that physical programs have a direct influence on improving a child's ability to read, spell, and perform other academic tasks; such statements lack evidence to support these claims.

As stated earlier, ridicule and exclusion from games, even at a young age, becomes a significant problem. Forced exclusion by peers often leads to self-exclusion or minimum participation. Participation and success in physical activity increases the likelihood that physical activity will be continued into adulthood. We are aware that regular healthy activity can contribute to the prevention of complaints such as obesity, heart disease, and osteoporosis, and exercise is an excellent tool for stress relief.

Accidents in the workplace and home are likely to be less if people are well coordinated. Good judgment, balance, and spatial skills decrease the likelihood of injury in activities such as climbing, balancing, or handling machinery and tools.

Driving skills, which many of us take for granted, may be more demanding for individuals who have difficulties in judging speed and spatial elements and experience slower reaction times. Consider this the next time someone pulls out in front of you and you can't understand why, or when you are impatiently sitting behind a car at a stop sign and the driver seems reluctant to pull out into traffic unless there is virtually a mile-long gap. Typically people with coordination difficulties *may* be more likely to make poor decisions or display slower and inappropriate reactions in busy traffic situations, especially in emergency situations.

We have a smorgasbord of choices in social and recreational activities at our disposal. This choice and/or at least the success in these activities potentially diminish depending on the level of coordination difficulties that an individual experiences. People may choose not to engage in recreational activities but the benefits—socially and physically—that can be derived from such activities are positive and rewarding. No individual should be denied the chance to participate and enjoy these activities because his or her coordination has been neglected in childhood.

Decreased occupational opportunities is another scenario for people who have coordination difficulties in either the fine or gross motor domain. Consider the number of people who are employed but then are dismissed for not being able to complete tasks accurately or quickly enough because of coordination difficulties. Imagine the frustration of individuals who have the academic aptitude to be a surgeon or a dentist, or the desire to be in electronics, but experience manipulative difficulties. Even a potential employee's physical appearance may create a biased impression of that person's work capabilities.

It has also been suggested by some medical professionals that for many people, sporting injuries—especially back, knee and muscular injuries—are due to poor running and other movement techniques, as well as a lack of flexibility not taught correctly or practiced from a young age. *Many children slowly and continuously damage their joints through exposure to incorrect techniques, especially in running, landing, and throwing movements.*

Uncoordinated children who grow up having had their movement difficulties ignored are more likely to become uncoordinated adults, who often tend not to encourage or play an active part in the physical development of their own children. Apart from the obvious negative physical impact, these parents have potentially lost a strong medium for bonding with their children in a fun and healthy way.

STRATEGIES FOR IDENTIFYING AND HELPING "CHILDREN AT RISK"

➤ Raise the awareness as to the importance of being physically coordinated. Create a "want" among teachers and parents to learn and understand the implications for children who are uncoordinated.

➤ Introduce a reliable screening tool in schools for identifying children at risk and provide computerized analysis of the data to enhance expediency. (See *Stay in Step*, Resource Index)

➤ Educate teachers in qualitative movement assessment skills and tools. (See *Fundamental Movement Skills Computer Assessment Program*, Resource Index)

➤ Provide a remediation resource to link teacher, parent, and child at risk.

➤ Train parents in fundamental movement skills to assist in movement enrichment programs during school time.

➤ Use parents as tutors, working at home with their own children.

➤ Allocate extra physical education time to these children at risk.

POINTER CUE CARDS

STATIC BALANCE

Teachable Points:

1. Head is up and the eyes are focused straight ahead on a fixed point.

2. Feet are flat on the floor with toes extended.

3. All body parts are kept straight and still.

4. Knees are kept slightly flexed.

5. Arms can be used to assist in balancing.

STATIC BALANCE

Common Faults:

1. Toes curled up.

2. Too much forward leaning at the hips.

3. Poor back and shoulder posture.

4. Excessive movement in body parts.

5. Balanced position too easily given up.

6. Head too far downward.

7. Too slow to make adjustments or over-compensate with their adjustments.

DYNAMIC BALANCE

Teachable Points:

1. Head up and eyes looking forward.

2. Back and shoulders are straight.

3. Body parts remain steady (no excessive wobble).

4. Feet are placed relatively straight along the walking path.

5. Knees are slightly flexed and the hips are straight.

6. Arms are held out, away from the body to assist balance.

DYNAMIC BALANCE

Common Faults:

1. Toes curled up.

2. Too much forward leaning at the hips.

3. Excessive movement in body parts.

4. Poor back and shoulder posture.

5. Head moving and eyes looking downward.

6. Balanced position too easily given up.

7. Too slow to make adjustments or over-compensate with their adjustments.

HORIZONTAL JUMP

Teachable Points:

1. Head up with eyes looking upward.

2. Arms extend behind the body as the knees and ankles bend.

3. At the same time, upper body bends forward at the hips.

4. Legs extend forcefully.

5. Jump is evenly off both feet.

6. The arm action is strong and synchronized with the leg action.

7. Body extends upward and forward.

HORIZONTAL JUMP

Common Faults:

1. Jumping more off one foot than the other.

2. Push with the legs is not quick or strong enough.

3. Not leaning forward prior to take-off.

4. Weak arm action.

5. Arms not swung up and forward.

6. Arms not synchronized with leg action.

7. Incorrect take-off angle.

8. Head down and eyes not looking forward.

LANDINGS

Teachable Points:

1. On landing, head is up with eyes looking forward.

2. On landing, lean slightly forward at the hips.

3. Arms are held out in front or to side of body to assist balance.

4. Land on balls of both feet and then roll back onto flat feet.

5. Ankles, knees, and hips bend to absorb force.

6. Feet should be shoulder-width apart.

LANDINGS

Common Faults:

1. Landing flat-footed, resulting in jarring.

2. Feet too close together causing over-balance.

3. Knees too straight, causing jarring and loss of balance.

4. Dropping head causing rotation and loss of balance.

VERTICAL JUMP

Teachable Points:

1. Head is up with eyes looking upward.

2. Arms extend behind the body as the knees and ankles bend.

3. At the same time, upper body bends forward at the hips.

4. Legs extend forcefully.

5. Jump is evenly off both feet.

6. The arms extend upward forcefully.

7. The arm action is synchronized with the leg action.

8. Body extends upward.

VERTICAL JUMP

Common Faults:

1. Jumping more off one foot than the other.

2. Push with the legs is not quick or strong enough.

3. Not leaning forward prior to take-off.

4. Weak arm action.

5. Arms not swung up and forward.

6. Arms not synchronized with leg action.

7. Incorrect take-off angle.

WALKING

Teachable Points:

1. Head is up and eyes looking in the direction of walking.

2. Body and limbs move in a straight line in the direction of the movement.

3. Feet are straight when in contact with the ground (not turned in or out).

4. Arms are slightly bent at the elbow.

5. Hands are relaxed.

6. Arms drive actively in opposition to the swinging leg.

7. Child lands on the heel, then moves up onto the toes.

WALKING

Common Faults:

1. Steps taken are too short.

2. Feet turned too far outward.

3. Walking on toes instead of heel–toe movement.

4. Landing too heavily.

5. Arms not moving in opposition to the legs.

6. Hands clenched in a fist, creating too much tension.

7. Head moving and the eyes not facing forward.

8. Jerky walking action.

RUNNING

Teachable Points:

1. Head remains up, with eyes looking forward in the direction of the movement.
2. Feet and legs move in a straight line in the direction of movement.
3. Arms are bent 90° at the elbow.
4. Arms drive actively in opposition to the legs.
5. Knee lift is close to right angles during the recovery phase.
6. Both feet are off the ground for a brief time.
7. Body is leaning slightly forward.
8. For sprint running, the supporting leg lands on the forefoot.

RUNNING

Common Faults:

1. Poor drive and push off the forefoot.
2. Length of the step is too small.
3. Legs and arms not moving straight forward, but outward, or across the body, causing too much upper body movement.
4. Flat-footed running.
5. The foot being placed on the ground pointing outward.
6. Non-support leg does not flex sufficiently toward the buttock; therefore, the knee lift becomes too low.
7. Trunk too upright or too far forward.
8. The arms are not flexed enough (less than 90° at the elbows).
9. Arms not moving in opposition to the legs.
10. Head moving and the eyes are not facing forward.

DODGING

Teachable Points:

1. Head is up and the eyes are focused straight ahead in the direction movement.
2. Change of direction is initiated by pushing off with the outside foot.
3. Push-off is forceful.
4. The knee of the supporting leg is bent as the direction change occurs.
5. The body is lowered during the direction change.
6. Balance is maintained.
7. Change of direction occurs quickly in one step.

DODGING

Common Faults:

1. Eyes wander instead of staying focused in direction of travel.
2. Body stays too upright.
3. Not enough push off the outside of the foot.
4. More than one step is taken to create change direction.
5. Loss of body control and falls over.
6. Changes of direction occur too slowly.

HOPPING

Teachable Points:

1. Head remains up and still with the eyes looking forward.
2. Knee of the non-supporting leg swings to produce force.
3. The foot is held behind the body.
4. Arms bent at 90° move actively in opposition to the driving leg.
5. Take-off and landing are on the forefoot.
6. Weight moves from the forefoot to the heel on landing.
7. Hopping leg bends to absorb the landing force.

HOPPING

Common Faults:

1. Landing flat-footed or staying on the toes.
2. Taking off flat-footed.
3. Non-support leg too low.
4. Poor leg drive.
5. Leaning too far forward or sideways.
6. Excessive upper body movement.
7. No arm drive.
8. Head moves or the eyes are looking down.

SKIPPING

Teachable Points:

1. Head remains up with eyes looking forward during the action.
2. Step-hop is evident.
3. Height and distance of steps and hops are consistent.
4. Body lean is correct.
5. Landing is on the forefoot.
6. Arms move in opposition to the legs.

SKIPPING

Common Faults:

1. Landing too flat-footed and heavy.
2. Inconsistent heights and distances of hops and steps.
3. Cannot hop; therefore, cannot skip.
4. Swing leg too high off the ground.
5. Poor balance.
6. Too much forward lean of the body.
7. Arms not synchronized in opposition with the legs.
8. Moving the head during the action.

LEAPING

Teachable Points:

1. Head remains up with eyes looking forward during the action.

2. Arms assist and are synchronized in opposition to the legs.

3. Take-off is on one foot; landing is on opposite foot.

4. Landing is on the forefoot.

5. Knee(s) bend slightly to absorb force on landing.

6. Balance is maintained on landing.

LEAPING

Common Faults:

1. Landing is too flat-footed and heavy.

2. Too much forward lean of the body.

3. Arms not synchronized in opposition with the legs when continuously leaping.

4. Poor balance.

5. Moving the head during the action.

SLIDE-STEPPING

Teachable Points:

1. Head is held up, still, and eyes looking in the direction of travel.

2. A step and then a slide are evident.

3. Width of slide-step is not too wide or too narrow.

4. Slide-step is on the forefoot.

5. Knees are slightly bent throughout the action.

6. Body is side-on.

7. Arms remain passive.

8. Child can slide both ways.

SLIDE-STEPPING

Common Faults:

1. Moving flat-footed.

2. Crossing feet because child leads with the wrong foot.

3. Slide-stepping too wide or narrow.

4. Leaping too high.

5. Legs too straight.

6. Arms making unwanted movements.

7. Turning the trunk and/or feet to face the direction of travel.

RECEIVING A ROLLED BALL

Teachable Points:

1. Eyes are focused on the ball source and track the ball along the ground.

2. Child moves to get the body behind the ball.

3. Fingers are spread and face downward ready to receive the oncoming ball.

4. Preferred leg is in front and knees bend to get down to the ball.

5. Child takes the ball cleanly in the hands.

RECEIVING A ROLLED BALL

Common Faults:

1. In an attempt to get down to the ball, child bends just from the waist without bending the knees.

2. Poor positioning of the body and hands in relation to the oncoming ball (not behind the ball).

3. Too much tension in the hands and fingers.

4. Fingers are not facing down to the ground.

5. Hands close too slowly or too quickly.

6. Not following the ball path or moving the eyes.

BOUNCE AND CATCH

Teachable Points:

1. Child keeps in a balanced position with the feet comfortably spaced.

2. Eyes are focused on the ball at all times.

3. Ball is pushed down with both hands by extending arms downward. (Does not "drop" the ball.)

4. Arms bend to receive oncoming ball at waist height.

5. Ball is caught at the sides with the fingers relaxed and spread (not patted).

6. When the ball meets the hands, arms bend at the elbows and cushion the impact of the ball.

BOUNCE AND CATCH

Common Faults:

1. Poor stability because stance is too narrow.

2. Poor positioning of the feet and hands in relation to the oncoming ball.

3. Ball is trapped against the body.

4. Continually alters height of body; especially bending excessively at the waist.

5. Elbows do not bend and therefore no give with the ball to absorb force.

6. Hands and fingers are poorly shaped.

7. Too much tension in the hands and fingers.

8. Hands close too slowly or at the wrong time.

9. Ball is patted rather than caught.

10. Ball is dropped passively rather than actively bounced.

11. Not following the ball or moving eyes and head away at impact.

CATCHING A LARGE BALL

Teachable Points:

1. Child is in a well balanced "ready" position (elbows slightly bent and fingers curved and spread).

2. Eyes are focused on the ball.

3. Arms move to meet the ball.

4. Hands are adjusted for the size of the ball.

5. Fingers face upward for a high ball; downward for a low ball.

6. Ball is cushioned on impact.

7. Ball is caught with the hands, not the arms trapping the ball against the body.

CATCHING A LARGE BALL

Common Faults:

1. Poor balance.

2. Poor positioning of the body and hands in relation to oncoming ball (not behind the ball).

3. Ball is trapped against the body.

4. Arms are not extended toward the ball.

5. No bending at elbows to absorb force.

6. Hands and fingers are poorly shaped.

7. Hands close too slowly or too quickly.

8. Too much tension in the hands and fingers before and during impact.

9. Makes no hand position adjustments according to the path of the ball.

10. Hands too wide apart to receive ball correctly.

11. Clapping at ball in attempt to catch it.

12. Not following ball flight or moving eyes and head away at impact.

CATCHING A SMALL BALL

Teachable Points:

1. Child is in a well-balanced "ready" position (elbows slightly bent and fingers curved and spread).

2. Eyes are focused on the ball.

3. Hands move to meet the ball.

4. Hands are adjusted for the size of the ball.

5. Fingers face upward for a high ball; downward for a low ball.

6. Ball is cushioned on impact.

7. Ball is caught correctly (not clapping it or trapping it against the body).

CATCHING A SMALL BALL

Common Faults:

1. Poor stability because stance is too narrow.

2. Poor positioning of the feet and hands in relation to the oncoming ball.

3. Ball is trapped against the body.

4. Continually alters height of body; especially bending excessively at the waist.

5. Elbows do not bend and therefore no give with the ball to absorb force.

6. Hands and fingers are poorly shaped.

7. Too much tension in the hands and fingers.

8. Hands close too slowly or at the wrong time.

9. Ball is patted rather than caught.

10. Ball is dropped passively rather than actively bounced.

11. Not following the ball or moving eyes and head away at impact.

BOUNCING A BALL

Teachable Points:

1. Child stands in a balanced position with feet comfortably spread.

2. Eyes are focused on the ball. When the skill increases, the eyes can look away from the ball.

3. Ball is pushed down with hand by extending arm downward.

4. Child must be ready to receive the bouncing ball, in ready position, elbow slightly bent.

5. Fingers are curved and spread.

6. Ball is bounced in front of and to side of the body.

BOUNCING A BALL

Common Faults:

1. Poor balance due to narrow stance.

2. Arm does not extend downward, but stays rigid.

3. Arm does not give slightly upward as ball contacts hands.

4. Elbow does not bend, and therefore no give with the ball to absorb force.

5. Hands and fingers are poorly shaped.

6. Ball is patted or slapped rather than pushed down off the fingers.

7. Too much tension in the hands, wrist, and fingers.

8. Hand closes too slowly or at the wrong time.

9. Eyes are not focused on the ball or just in front of the ball.

UNDERHAND THROW

Teachable Points:

1. Child starts in a balanced position with feet comfortably spread and faces the target.

2. Eyes are focused on the target.

3. Ball is held mainly in the fingers.

4. Weight transference occurs quickly by stepping forward with the foot opposite to the throwing arm.

5. Good arm extension in the wind-up.

6. Throw starts with the hips rotating toward the target.

7. Ball is released in front of the body (not too early or too late).

8. Good extension in the follow-through which is in the direction of the target.

UNDERHAND THROW

Common Faults:

1. Poor balance.

2. Incorrect foot forward.

3. Poor weight transfer in backward and forward throwing phases.

4. Ball held in the palm rather than fingers.

5. Arm does not extend on backward arm action.

6. Poor timing of release (too soon or too late).

7. Poor follow-through.

8. Not focusing the eyes on the target.

OVERHAND THROW

Teachable Points:

1. Child starts in a balanced position side-on to the target.
2. Eyes are focused on the target.
3. Ball is held at the base of the fingers.
4. Weight transference by stepping forward with foot opposite to throwing arm.
5. Good arm extension is evident.
6. Wrist is cocked at the back of the wind-up.
7. Throw starts with the hips rotating toward the target and then the shoulders follow.
8. As the arm moves forward, it bends approximately 90°.
9. Arm extends full again at ball release.
10. Ball is released in front of the body.
11. Wrist snaps downward.
12. Good extension in follow-through toward target, then down and past leg.

OVERHAND THROW

Common Faults:

1. Poor balance.
2. Incorrect foot forward.
3. Poor weight transfer in backward and forward throwing phases.
4. Ball held in the palm rather than fingers.
5. Arm does not extend on backward arm action.
6. Poor timing of release (too soon or too late).
7. Poor follow-through.
8. Not focusing the eyes on the target.

SINGLE-HANDED STRIKING

Teachable Points:

1. Child stands balanced with feet apart in the ready position.
2. Eyes are focused.
3. The striking hand extends backward until nearly straight.
4. Weight transfers forward by stepping into the swing with the foot opposite the striking hand.
5. Side-on hitting position is obtained.
6. The head of the racquet is kept slightly above the wrist and the wrist is held firm.
7. Forward swing starts with rotation of the hips followed by the shoulders.
8. Follow-through is in the intended direction.
9. Ball is struck opposite the front foot.

SINGLE-HANDED STRIKING

Common Faults:

1. Poor balance due to a narrow stance.
2. Not standing side-on.
3. Not transferring weight.
4. Insufficient shoulder turn.
5. Getting too close to the ball; cramping the arm action.
6. Swinging upward instead of forward.
7. Bending the hitting arm excessively.
8. Dropping the wrist or wrist too loose.
9. Poor follow-through.
10. Head moves and/or eyes are not focused on the ball.

TWO-HANDED STRIKING

Teachable Points:

1. Eyes are focused on the ball, head steady.
2. Child stands in a sideways position.
3. Weight transference occurs back and then forward (e.g., in T-Ball, by stepping into the hit).
4. Good shoulder turn in backswing.
5. Non-preferred arm remains relatively straight in backswing.
6. Hit starts with the hips rotating toward the target.
7. Knees remain flexed during the hit.
8. Good extension in the follow-through is evident.

TWO-HANDED STRIKING

Common Faults:

1. Poor balance due to narrow stance or standing stiff-legged.
2. Not standing side-on.
3. Straightening the knees especially on the downswing.
4. Going up on the toes on the downswing.
5. Wrong hand position on the bat.
6. Insufficient shoulder turn.
7. Excessively bending the non-preferred arm.
8. Does not start the downswing with the hips.
9. Lack of follow-through.
10. Eyes not focused on the ball.

KICKING FOR DISTANCE

Teachable Points:

1. Eyes focused on the ball.
2. Step is forward with the non-kicking foot placed close to the ball.
3. Balance is maintained throughout kicking action.
4. Adequate bending of the kicking leg's knee in backswing is evident.
5. Ball is contacted on the instep of the kicking foot.
6. Arm opposite the kicking leg moves forward during the kick.
7. Good extension in the follow-through in the direction of the target occurs.

KICKING FOR DISTANCE

Common Faults:

1. Poor balance.
2. Placing the non-kicking foot too close to the ball.
3. Not bending the kicking leg enough.
4. Kicking with the toe instead of the instep.
5. Poor use of the opposite arm to assist balance.
6. Striking the ball off center.
7. Follow-through is incomplete.
8. Follow-through is around the body.
9. Head moves or eyes are taken off the ball.

KICKING FOR ACCURACY

Teachable Points:

1. Eyes are focused on the ball.

2. Step is into the correct position with the non-kicking foot placed close to the ball.

3. Adequate backswing of the kicking leg is evident.

4. Ball is contacted on the inside of the kicking foot.

5. Balance is maintained throughout kicking action.

6. Good extension in the follow-through in the direction of the target occurs.

KICKING FOR ACCURACY

Common Faults:

1. Head moves or eyes are taken off the ball.

2. Non-kicking foot is placed too close to the ball.

3. Not kicking with the side of the foot.

4. Poor use of the arms.

5. Striking the ball off center.

6. Follow-through is incomplete.

7. Follow-through is around the body.

PUNT KICKING

Teachable Points:

1. Eyes are focused on the ball.

2. Step is forward onto non-kicking foot.

3. Ball is held correctly in front of body at hip height with both hands.

4. Adequate bending of the kicking leg's knee in backswing (at least 90°).

5. Ball is guided down with the hand on the same side as kicking leg (not dropped).

6. Ball is contacted on the instep of the kicking foot.

7. Arm opposite the kicking leg moves forward during the kick.

8. High follow-through occurs in the direction of the target.

PUNT KICKING

Common Faults:

1. Not running straight at the target.

2. Not bending the kicking leg enough on the backswing.

3. Kicking with the toe instead of instep.

4. Striking the ball off center.

5. Inaccurate dropping of the ball.

6. The opposite arm not assisting in balance.

7. Follow-through is too low.

8. Follow-through is not straight but is around the body.

9. Ball is dropped by both hands and not guided down.

10. Head moves or eyes are taken off the ball.

RESOURCES INDEX

The following resources both complement and supplement the *Ready-to-Use Fundamental Motor Skills & Movement Activities for Young Children*:

- *Complete Physical Education Activities Program* (K-9), Joanne M. Landy and Maxwell J. Landy (Paramus, NJ: *Prentice Hall* 1993).

- *50 Simple Ways to Raise a Child Who Is Physically Fit*, Joanne M. Landy and Keith R. Burridge (New York: *Macmillan* 1997).

- *Complete Motor Skills Activities Program*, Joanne M. Landy and Keith R. Burridge (West Nyack, NY: *The Center for Applied Research in Education* 1999).

- *Stay in Step: A Gross Motor Screening Test for Children K-2*, Dr. Dawne Larkin and Gay Revie (1994).

- *Fundamental Movement Skills Computer Assessment Package*, Keith R. Burridge and Joanne M. Landy (1998).

Available through SPORTIME and the authors.